This is a **FLAME TREE** book
First published in 2008

Publisher and Creative Director: Nick Wells
Project Editor: Cat Emslie
Art Director and Layout Design: Mike Spender
Digital Design and Production: Chris Herbert
Picture Research: Cat Emslie, Toria Lyle
Proofreader: Daniela Nava
Indexer: William Jack

Special thanks to Chelsea Edwards and Sara Robson

10 12 11 09
3 5 7 9 10 8 6 4 2

This edition first published 2008 by
FLAME TREE PUBLISHING
Crabtree Hall, Crabtree Lane
Fulham, London SW6 6TY
United Kingdom

www.flametreepublishing.com

Flame Tree is part of the Foundry Creative Media Co. Ltd
© 2008 this edition the Foundry Creative Media Co. Ltd

ISBN 978-1-84786-399-7

A CIP Record for this book is available from the British Library upon request

Printed in India

All pictures are courtesy of Shutterstock and © the following photographers: 5t & 16, 204 Yellowj; 5b & 42 First Class Photos PTY LTD; 6c & 100 rep0rter; 6b & 120, 11, 19, 41, 49, 59, 61, 65, 75, 76, 78, 80, 97, 104, 154, 161, 199, 226, 230 Monkey Business Images; 6t & 70 Viktor1; 7t & 140 Knud Nielsen; 7c & 168 Apollofoto; 7b & 192 Petr Jilek; 8t & 212 Baevskiy Dmitry; 8b & 232 Dusan Zidar; 10 Ivanastar; 12 Mark William Richardson; 15 egd; 18 Kinetic Imagery; 21 Zsolt Nyulaszi; 22 digitalife; 23, 35 Dmitriy Shironosov; 25 Igor Smichkov; 28 silver-john; 29 Milos Jokic; 30 Valery Potapova; 33 Mikael Damkier; 34 Fotocrisis; 36, 219 Graca Victoria; 38 Keith A Frith; 45 Stephen Coburn; 48, 89, 117 iofoto; 54 Adrian Britton; 57 Podfoto; 67 kotik1; 68 Radu Razvan; 77 Morgan Lane Photography; 79 Heather Evans; 81 Rene Jansa; 83 Olga Chernetskaya; 85 Carl Southerland; 87 Ingvald Kaldhussater; 88 Maceofoto; 91 Steve Lovegrove; 92b Andrew G. Davis; 92t David Hughes; 93 bravajulia; 98 Diego Cervo; 99 Jamzol; 103 Jennifer Nickert; 108 Zastol'skiy Victor Leonidovich; 110 Suzanne Tucker; 111 Gina Smith; 114 luxe; 120 Joe Gough; 123 Kameel4u; 127, 143, 169 Andresr; 130 Milkos; 132b Richard Sargeant; 132t Michael Pettigrew; 136 TheSupe87; 139 Norman Chan; 140 GeoM; 147 Andrejs Pidjass; 148, 234 Yuri Arcurs; 151 Foxie; 152 Konstantin Sutyagin; 156 Lein de Léon Yong; 159 Helder Almeida; 162 Oleg V. Ivanov; 165 Trevor Allen; 166 Tatiana Popova; 171, 242 Johann Helgason; 175, 177 Nikolay Okhitin; 178 2734725246; 179 Perov Stanislav; 181 Stephen Strathdee; 182 Fred Sweet; 185 Ethan Andrews; 189 Vladimir Mucibabic; 191 Douglas Freer; 192 Mr Klein; 196 Stanislav Sokolov; 201 Darren Baker; 205 Nobor; 206 Plotnikov M; 209 Lincoln Rogers; 210 1125089601; 215 Orange line Media; 216 Kurhan; 220 Andre Blais; 221 Karen Roach; 223 Ivan Cholakov; 225 vhpfoto; 236 Losevsky Pavel; 237 Sergei Didyk; 239 Losevsky Pavel; 241 RoJo Images; 246 prism_68; 248 Svetlana Larina; 251 Carlos Arranz

Beat the Credit Crunch

Shopping

Foreword: Pauline McCallion

Andrea Dean
Gráinne Gilmore
Simoney Girard
Mike Naylor
Laura Shannon
Hannah Smith

on a

Budget

FLAME TREE
PUBLISHING

Contents

Price Comparison Websites

The more the internet continues to go grow as a shopping destination, the more entrepreneurs will cater to our desire to avoid trawling though a hundred websites looking for the best deal on energy utilities or a new camera. This chapter is devoted to explaining how comparison websites work, how to choose which ones to use and how to get the best out of them.

Discounts & General Shopping

There are many ways to get discounts and reductions on your shopping, including vouchers and coupons in magazines and online, cashback from websites and credit cards, loyalty cards, store cards, haggling, auctions, TV shopping, discount stores and sales shopping. All this and more is covered here.

Food Shopping

Though we all have to eat, there are many ways we can cut the cost without resorting to beans on toast every day. The supermarkets are waging a price war on each other to fight for your custom. Learn how to pick through the maze, get the best deals on offer and find the best places to shop – for anything from value brands and the new discount supermarkets to pound shops and markets.

Household

Keeping your house spic and span needn't cost the earth. This chapter provides invaluable advice on shopping for cleaning products – for example buying own-brand and in bulk. Also covered is how to buy furniture, furnishings, housewares and DIY products on a budget, as well as kit out your kitchen and bathroom without breaking the bank.

Appliances & Electronics

We could certainly do without many of the gadgets we buy and use only once, but there are also certain items that we would consider necessities, such as most white goods, toasters and kettles, televisions, DVD players and even computers. This section shows you how to decide what you need, where to get it and how to beat the price down.

144 ——— Clothes & Accessories

Clothes shopping is many a girl's vice, but it is something that must be reined in during leaner times. However, a little retail therapy will not go amiss – discover how to slash your garment spending on the high street, online, abroad and on catalogues. Not forgetting hiring special outfits and nabbing second-hand vintage bargains.

Travel ——————— 172

Fuel costs are spiralling, making driving even more expensive. But if you can't bear to lose the car we show you how to reduce spending on insurance, breakdown cover and petrol. Getting the best deals on flights, trains, car hire, insurance and travel money is also covered.

194 ——— Services & Utilities

Gas and electricity prices keep rising so it's more important than ever to make sure you are on the right deal. This section provides guidance on switching utilities and even saving money on water. The maze of phone, mobile and broadband packages is explored too, as is the raft of financial services – how to get the best out of your banking, loans, credit cards and insurance.

Sport & Leisure ——— 212

Shopping for sport and leisure is yet another area where you can cut back on spending without neglecting your health or social life. Sports gear, gym membership, nights out, tickets for entertainment and dining out are just some of the items you can bag at much lower prices than you realize.

232 ——————— Gifts

Shopping for gifts can be an unplanned-for expenditure that makes the difference between strapped-for-cash and thoroughly skint. But there is no need to do your friends and family out of their birthday presents – just follow the advice given here on gift shopping on the cheap, from online to supermarkets. With a little thinking outside the box, ideas are suggested for all gift-giving occasions.

Foreword

In the late summer of 2007, it was difficult to open a paper or turn on the television without being confronted by images of Northern Rock customers queuing outside the bank's branches to withdraw their life savings. This was the first run on a British bank in more than a century and it was at this point that reality began to hit home for the UK. The era of easy borrowing had finally come to an end.

Over the past five to 10 years, borrowers have been bombarded with endless offers for 0 per cent credit card deals and attractive loans and mortgages. While this activity promoted competition between providers and helped the UK personal finance sector become one of the most innovative in the world, with hindsight the market was obviously heading for a massive fall.

The global financial crisis now generally known as the 'credit crunch' actually kicked off across the pond. A rash of US lenders indiscriminately offered enticing loans with cheap opening rates to borrowers. But when the initial deal ended, interest rates shot up, financially crippling households across America. The problem seeped onto the world stage because packages of these loans had been bundled up and sold on as investments to other financial organizations. Once borrowers started to struggle to meet their repayments, interest in buying these packages of loans soon dried up – unsurprisingly, no organization was willing to risk purchasing a bundle of loans that could potentially go bad.

Meanwhile, UK lenders had been selling bundles of their own loans. Once investment interest dried up, those relying too much on this method, such as Northern Rock, found they had nowhere to turn in order to fund their lending to consumers. This scarcity of funding consequently forced up interest rates on mortgages and loans, bringing us to the present day, where lenders with severely reduced product ranges are cautious about even the most financially healthy loan applicants.

Add rising food and energy prices to the mix and it's clear that UK consumers now need to rein in their spending and become more sensible about saving and borrowing. Thankfully, there is lots of scope for shopping around and this book should provide inspiration on how to bag a bargain, whether you're looking for a new television, hoping to reduce your gas bill, or even shopping for your groceries.

Pauline McCallion
Editor
Your Mortgage and *Your Money*

Introduction

Have you noticed the cost of your weekly food shop seems to be creeping up? Are you struggling with payments as the interest rate on your mortgage or credit card inches higher? Are you a motorist finding it more and more costly to put petrol in your car? You are a victim of the credit crunch. You may feel the pain in your pocket, but do you really understand how the UK economy and much of the Western world came to be in this difficult situation?

Origins

It can all be traced back to the US mortgage market. Over the last few years when credit was cheap and business was booming, the big US banks were lending to consumers freely and with abandon. The banks sold each other packages of debt from sub-prime borrowers, meaning those with low credit ratings who were most at risk of missing payments. This irresponsible lending by the giant financials finally came home to roost when many borrowers did default on their home loans.

A year on from the start of the trouble, the banks have been forced to write off billions of dollars between them. To recoup these losses, they have tightened their lending criteria and pushed up interest rates on mortgages so other forms of credit and now customers have begun to feel the pinch. There has been a ripple effect across the globe, as most of the big banks are businesses with international operations.

Ripples on Both Sides of the Pond

As the ripple reached the UK, consumers suffered and as a consequence so did retailers since people cut down their household spending. In a bid to stimulate the sluggish economy, the Bank of England cut interest rates, albeit much less aggressively than the US Federal Reserve, allowing inflation to rise in the process. This is why many families' weekly shopping bill has hit the roof, motorists are struggling to run their cars and people across the country dread the arrival of the monthly gas bill.

Companies have suffered along with consumers. In the US, investment bank Bear Stearns collapsed despite an emergency bail out attempt by the Federal Reserve. This was a direct result of the sub-prime lending crisis. In the UK, the dramatic demise of Northern Rock was the clearest indicator that something was very wrong in the mortgage market. The government had to bail out the stricken lender while its panicked customers queued outside the bank's branches for hours trying to withdraw their savings.

Mortgage Difficulties

Homeowners and first time buyers have been hit particularly hard by the effects of the credit crunch. It is now very difficult to get a mortgage unless you have a spotless credit rating and a very large deposit – 20 or 25 per cent in some cases – and even then there are no guarantees it will be a competitive deal. Banks have been burned and are now extremely reluctant to take even the slightest risk of default on payments. Many have pulled their best mortgage deals out of the marketplace altogether. This has priced potential buyers out of the market, ironically at a time when house prices have fallen so low that they are now more affordable than ever.

The situation is becoming increasingly perilous for those who already own their homes. House prices continue to fall, with some industry experts predicting they will have dropped by a quarter before they start to recover. This means the equity nest egg many people were relying on for their financial security in retirement is rapidly dwindling. Those with fixed rate mortgages that are coming to an end are having to shift to variable rate deals which are much less favourable, pushing up their monthly repayments. As a direct result, repossessions are soaring and many people have been forced to sell to unscrupulous lenders for a song and then rent their homes back to avoid losing them altogether.

This combined with high levels of individual consumer debt – the result of our 'buy now, pay later' spending culture – has driven many to the brink of bankruptcy.

Taking Advantage of the Credit Crunch

Amid all this doom and gloom, there are things that could work in your favour. Retailers are feeling the pinch as consumer spending slows and many are lowering prices and offering great deals to lure customers in an increasingly competitive environment.

Supermarkets are slashing the prices of basic groceries and many high street stores are extending their seasonal sales. Some shops are also starting to offer more spot discounts on individual items, as well as providing greater enticements to buy in bulk, with two-for-one and buy-one-get-one-free promotions becoming more and more common. Shrewd consumers can take advantage of this, and this book shows you how.

Shopping Benefits

The food shopping chapter in this book covers supermarkets, including loyalty schemes, in-store offers and reductions, buying own-brand and no-frills products, and discount supermarkets such as Aldi and Lidl. You can also discover the pros and cons of farmers' markets and buying organic, and how to make the most of the internet to cut your shopping spend.

The section on cars and travel gives you tips on reducing your car insurance premium and breakdown cover, and saving on fuel as prices rise. When you are heading further afield, we give you the inside track on cheap flights, travel insurance and foreign currency.

For gym bunnies, the chapter on sports and leisure steers you towards the best deals on gym membership, sports clothing and equipment and even extreme sports cover. And there's no need to stay glued to the couch even though you are on a budget. We show you how to go out on the town for very little money, including nightclubs, bars, comedy clubs, gigs, theatre and the cinema.

Shopaholics should check the clothes and accessories section for advice on seasonal sales, making store cards work to your advantage, second-hand clothes and the wonderful world of vintage.

To ensure every base is covered, see the chapters on general shopping and discounts of all shapes and sizes, economizing on household essentials and saving money on big ticket electronics and appliances. We also guide you through the plethora of price comparison websites, help you cut your utilities and phone bills, and suggest ways to penny-pinch on your Christmas gift shopping.

Price Comparison Websites

Background

The internet has revolutionized shopping, making a wide array of products and services from around the world available to you from the comfort of your own home. But some entrepreneurs realized that rather than making you visit the website of each and every retailer to compare the deals on offer, they could become the middleman, saving you legwork by letting you compare the prices of a host of similar products and services on one site.

First Appearance

Price comparison websites first appeared in the 1990s as the internet began to grow in popularity and became more far-reaching. Their creators also realized that such sites could be very lucrative, not through selling any of the products listed, but rather through commission

from retailers and suppliers, as well as additional income that could be generated by selling advertising on a popular site. The first examples of these sites were found in the US, but the UK soon followed suit with its own versions designed for the British public.

Today

A plethora of price comparison websites have now sprung up to make trawling the net for the best deals even easier, letting you source bargains with the minimum of effort, and it is estimated these sites are growing at an annual rate of 30 to 50 per cent in the UK. Whatever you are looking for – a mortgage, a holiday, some furniture or a new DVD player – there are a host of websites dedicated to letting you compare the deals available.

How They Collate Their Information

Each site uses different versions of the same technology so that they can source and provide up to date information as quickly as possible. This technology shares some of the same characteristics as that used by search engines in general. The efficiency and worth of each individual site comes down to how well it collects information. For any service to really be worth its salt, it has to update its prices daily, if not more frequently than that. Modern-day price comparison sites get their data from a number of different avenues. Typically they will combine different elements of the following options:

From the Retailers

The retailers provide the information themselves, giving links to the relevant pages on their own websites, giving delivery costs and including any promotions they are running.

Technology

They use data extraction technology to scour the net – these are sometimes called screenscraper sites.

Third Party

Some comparison sites access information about a wider range of retailers through a consolidated database provided by a third party.

Man-Hours

Each site will employ people to source new retailers and also to check the accuracy of the data that comes through.

Starting Your Search

Type the name of most items into a search engine such as Google or Ask and you will be presented with a plethora of options including price comparison sites, all vying for your attention. If you click the link through to a comparison site, you will then have the option to search through the product ranges of a variety of suppliers, with results usually presented in under a minute.

How to Choose

Which websites are the best? And what should you look out for when making your choice? The point of price comparison websites is to make life easier for you, but knowing a few facts about how they put together the information on display will help you negotiate your way round these sites and clinch the best deals in the shortest amount of time.

Find Out Which Companies They Cover

Some websites may be 'whole of market' – offering you a choice of deals from every supplier in that particular area such as, for example, every savings provider or electricity company. But others only offer prices from a selection of firms. For this reason it is often worth visiting several comparison sites before committing yourself to purchasing an item, or signing up for a new deal, as others may be quoting prices from different firms.

To get a better idea of which companies the price comparison site works with, look for the small print on the website. For example, www.moneysupermarket.co.uk, a website which compares the cost of all types of insurance, as well as motoring and travel among other areas, lists the companies not included in the quotes it offers at

www.moneysupermarket.com/c/customer-promise/companies-not-compared. uSwitch, another website, also lists the firms it does not cover in each area, and at the beginning of each section there is a link through to details on the criteria for including a supplier.

Look Out for Commercial Relationships

The vast majority of price comparison sites are free for you to use. But knowing a little about how the sites make their money is also useful when it comes to comparing deals. Comparison sites make money through payments from the retailers or suppliers who are listed on it. These companies will usually be charged in one of the following ways:

 Flat fee: A flat fee to cover a particular period of time

Fee per click: An individual fee every time a user clicks on the link through to the retailer's own website

Fee per purchase: A fee every time the user either buys something, or fills in their details on the site in order to find out more information

Look Past the Commercial Relationships

Most comparison sites are very clear about whether they will receive a fee if you click through to the supplier and some, especially those comparing financial products or utilities, will include prices from suppliers who they do not have a commercial relationship with, simply so they can offer you a wider choice of deals.

For example, uSwitch, the site best known for comparing gas and electricity prices, shows prices from most gas and electricity companies despite the fact that it does not receive a commission (of between £30 and £60) from all the companies if you then switch to their deal. The site offers visitors the choice of only seeing the suppliers with which they can set up a

new account immediately via its site – that is, the companies from whom it receives a commission – or you can see every supplier it includes in its lists, regardless of the commercial relationship. In the interests of doing your research fully, you should choose the latter option.

What's in a Price?

When looking at a price comparison site, try and establish if the price quoted is an example price or the exact amount you will have to pay. As the main purpose of price comparison sites is to cut down on the legwork you have to do and give you fast results, some sites, especially those specializing in quoting insurance premiums, will make assumptions about you to make the quote process faster. But this can often result in you receiving a quote which is only an estimate and which could actually increase once you contact the insurer to set up the cover. Basing your choice of cover on estimated prices could be a false economy. Also, make sure all the quotes you receive include VAT.

Categories

Price comparison websites fall into several separate categories, although there is some overlap between them. In general, however, if you are looking to find the best prices for a particular product, there will be a certain site that is better suited to the task. In broad terms, sites can be split into the categories discussed below. See also the other chapters in this book for more general advice on specific shopping areas.

Utility Providers

It used to be the case that people would sign up to an electricity or gas supplier and then stay with them for life. The concept of shopping around for the best price was not part of the national psyche and the sheer time and effort needed to change suppliers, if indeed it was even possible, made it unachievable for most people.

Times have changed. Individuals are no longer tied to one supplier and have the freedom to change in order to secure the best possible deal. This, in turn, has encouraged a healthier level of competition in the industry, which can only ever be a good thing for consumers.

Price Increases Lead to More Websites

As oil and gas prices soar and providers come under attack from consumer groups for implementing steep price hikes, while still enjoying huge profit margins, sourcing the best deals becomes more important than ever. A wide range of price comparison sites have been launched to make it easier than ever to check if you could save on your annual energy bills by checking all the deals available.

Overlap

Many price comparison sites started by concentrating on one area of the market, but have since branched out, offering comparison tools for other products, so in many cases you can look up the best broadband and phone deals too.

The Websites

The best sites to visit when comparing gas and electricity are those that have been given the seal of approval from Energywatch, the energy watchdog (for more information on Energywatch visit www.energywatch.co.uk). These are:

✅ **www.confused.com**: This site compares gas and electricity prices as well as broadband, phones and all types of insurance and finance. IT offers a £40 Virgin WineBank voucher for all those who change energy supplier via the site.

✅ **www.energyhelpline.com**: This website, which offers comparison tools for utilities as well as broadband, finance, broadband and a special section for businesses, offers up to £15 cashback for switching to some deals online, or via its phone line – 0800 074 0745.

✅ **www.energylinx.co.uk**: A specialist comparison service for gas and electricity covering the whole of the market. Customers can look at quotes for deals based on the price, customer service or green rating.

✅ **www.homeadvisoryservice.com**: This site compares a range of utilities and houshold expenses, including a handy guide to claiming refunds on your tax bill and reclaiming bank charge.

✅ **www.moneyexpert.com**: Gas and electricity deals are covered, as are all finance deals, including equity release and broadband.

✅ **www.moneysupermarket.com**: This is one of the biggest comparison sites, listing prices for gas and electricity and also comparing deals for all personal finances, such as savings and current accounts, as well as insurance.

✅ **www.switchandgive.com**: This utility comparison site is not on energywatch's list, but its calculator tool is powered by energyhelpline, which is on the list. If you would like to help a charity by switching your gas or energy supplier, then this is the site for you. It pays £30 to a charity for each customer that switches via the site.

✅ **www.switchwithwhich.co.uk**: This site concentrates on comparing gas and electricity prices, with useful information on grants available to help cover the cost of the bills. There is an online eligibilty checker to help you ascertain if you might be able to access a grant.

- **www.theenergyshop.com**: A dedicated gas and electricity comparison site.

- **www.ukpower.co.uk**: A specialist site for gas and electricity switching for households and businesses.

- **www.unravelit.com**: This site compares utility prices, home telephone, loans, credit cards and home insurance. This website claims to cover the whole of the market for energy providers, and the company behind the website also runs comparison tools for AOL, MSN and Tesco.

- **www.uswitch.com**: A large comparison site which not only includes gas and electricity, but all aspects of household expenses including insurance, heating cover, broadband and digital TV. It also has a comprehensive comparison tool for financial products.

Criteria to Bear in Mind

When choosing a gas or electricity deal, it is worth considering what criteria you are prepared to accept in order to achieve the best price. The price comparison websites generate quotes by using a series of calculators that look at factors such as the current price you are paying, where you live and the payment method you use. While you can obviously cut bills by using less energy, you could also save an average of £150 a year by switching to paying by direct debit each month rather than paying by cheque each quarter. Energywatch also says those who currently have a prepayment meter can save about £170 by choosing to pay by direct debit. However, if you are on a tight budget, consider this option carefully, as direct debit payments are often calculated using estimated billing, so you could pay more than you need to for several months in a row. One way around this however is to call your energy company with up to date meter readings on a regular basis.

Consider the Term of the Deal

Committing to a longer-term deal can also be beneficial, but bear in mind that many energy companies increased their tariffs by a third in the first six months of 2008 and more price rises are likely. In these circumstances, being locked into a deal may not be the best option, unless you choose a capped tariff, which guarantees the price will not rise above a certain level.

Think of the Environment

If your carbon footprint is also a concern, most websites have green tariff calculators, allowing you to compare deals not only on price but on their environmental credentials.

Financial Products

Gone are the days when you simply visited your bank manager when you wanted to open a savings account or apply for a credit card. Banks and building societies are more like high street shops these days, fighting tooth and nail for your custom. Shopping around for car, home and travel insurance has also become more

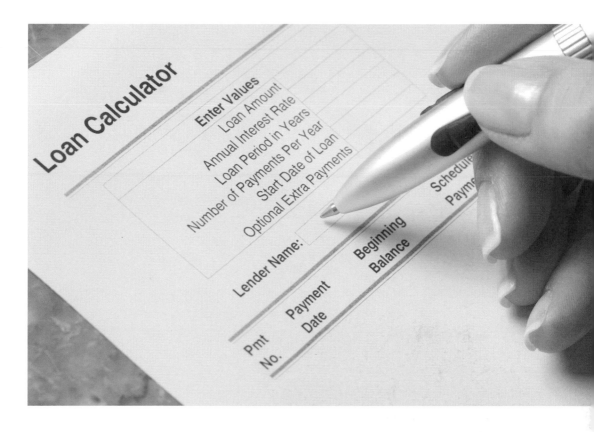

beneficial as insurers try to tempt new customers with attractive deals. In these credit crunched times, however, financial institutions are a lot keener to get your money (via savings, current and investment accounts) than to give it to you (via loans, mortgages or credit cards.)

Why Hunt for a Home Loan?

As the cost of living rises, it has never been more important to try and clinch the best deals available. Mortgage costs eat up the biggest chunk of most homeowners' monthly income and taking out a home loan which is even just a couple of percentage points more expensive than the best deal available to you could add hundreds of pounds to the cost of your annual bill. It can take more than two months to set up a new mortgage in some cases, so start looking at

new deals well before your current deal comes to an end to get an idea of some of the best rates available. Bear in mind that some lenders and mortgage brokers may have exclusive deals that are not registered on price comparison sites. But they are always a good place to start.

Clarify Your Credit Rating

If you are worried that your credit record may not be as unblemished as you would like, you should establish what your credit rating actually is. If you have a clean credit record, it is still fairly straightforward to get a loan deal, but if you have missed payments or even been declared insolvent in the past, you will not be accepted for some deals. Applying for a mortgage, personal loan or credit card and being turned down could leave a footprint on your credit record, which can actually result in your credit rating becoming less attractive.

How to check: You can check your credit file at www.checkmyfile.com, www.experian.co.uk, www.equifax.co.uk or www.callcredit.co.uk. These are not price comparison websites, but a visit to one of these sites should be a precursor to using any comparison website.

Moneysupermarket: One of the biggest finance sites, this also has a handy 'smart search' tool which asks questions to ascertain your credit profile and quotes deals that will suit you as a result.

Rate Tarts

The rise of price comparison sites for all aspects of finance has also ushered in the age of the 'rate tart'. These are savers or borrowers who sign up for the great deals offered by many banks and building societies to entice new customers. Traditionally, financial institutions could rely on their new customers staying put once the great deal came to an end. After all, there are still tens of thousands of savers who have accounts paying paltry rates of interest at the high street banks. But now, with the range of websites available to tell consumers about the best new deals, the latter are less willing to stay put and can switch to a rival bank once the original deal runs out. This form of switching is most beneficial when it comes to 0 per cent credit card deals, which charge no interest for a set amount of time, or savings accounts which offer an introductory bonus rate of interest for six or 12 months.

 Be a successful rate tart – set your alarm: The key to being a 'rate tart' is not being caught out when the deal comes to an end by making a note of the end date and switching to a new, attractive deal in good time. If you don't think a calendar or diary entry will be enough to remind you, use the 'tart alert' on Moneysavingexpert, the specialist site for saving money: www.moneysavingexpert.com/cards/credit-card-tart.

Visit Several Websites

The popularity of price comparison sites, especially when searching for a financial product, was underlined by a recent Which? report which showed that around 6.5 million people visited one of the three largest sites – www.moneysupermarket.com, www.gocompare.com and www.confused.com – during one month alone. But the consumer body also underlined the importance of widening your search to more than one price comparison site as it said that its research into insurance quotes found that some sites can show startlingly different prices for the same product. So it is worth visiting several sites and even contacting several insurers or lenders directly before making any decision about signing on the dotted line.

The Websites

Here are some of the best sites if you are looking for a new mortgage, a current account, a credit card, some home or car insurance, or another financial product:

 www.comparethemarket.com: Primarily a site for all types of insurance, including home, travel and car, but also includes details of personal loans, credit cards and other products such as breakdown cover and car hire insurance.

✔️ **www.confused.com**: This site, which started off as a car insurance comparison site, now encompasses credit cards, mortgages, car loans, personal loans and insurance – including life cover, small business insurance and wedding cover as well as pet insurance.

✔️ **www.defaqto.co.uk**: This site lists the most competitive deals for credit cards, loans, insurance, savings accounts, current accounts, pensions and investments.

✔️ **www.gocompare.com**: A comparison service for all types of insurance as well as money, motoring, travel and utilities

✔️ **www.fool.co.uk**: The Motley Fool offers price comparison tools for home loans, savings accounts, credit cards, current accounts, personal loans as well as car and life insurance.

✔️ **www.moneyfacts.co.uk**: This site compares prices for mortgages, savings accounts, current accounts, credit and store cards and personal loans as well as giving you home, car, health and life insurance quotes. Its best-buy tables give you an idea of the best deals available at a glance. It also includes the best deals for business bank accounts.

✔️ **www.moneymadeclear.fsa.gov.uk**: The Financial Services Authority operates this price comparison site which covers mortgages, pensions and investment bonds. It also has handy calculators to help you work out how much you will have to pay for your home loan or personal loan each month, as well as a pension calculator which will give you an indication of how much money you can expect to receive in retirement.

✔️ **www.moneysupermarket.com**: This site compares prices for all aspects of personal finances, including loans, credit cards, mortgages, savings, current accounts and debt consolidation loans. It also compares prices for car, home, travel and life insurance as

well as pet insurance, dental cover and breakdown cover. The website also has an 'ask the expert' section, where you can pose your thorny questions to one of the website's many specialists.

 www.uswitch.com: The site offers price comparison for gas and electricity as well as quotes for heating cover, water, mobile phones, broadband, home phones, digital TV, insurance and financial products such as credit cards. uSwitch also offers a customer services team to deal with enquiries.

Retail Websites

If you can't face the hordes of people on the high street, there is no reason why you can't shop online. Most stores now have an online presence, with many dedicating resources to make sure the sites are as easy to use as possible. Price comparison sites promise to cut your workload even further. After all, if you can save yourself trawling one retail website after another, you will have more time to sit back and enjoy your new purchases.

Groceries – mySupermarket

Many supermarkets now offer online shopping so you can order your groceries without leaving the comfort of your sofa. And if you want to make sure you are paying the least for your weekly shop, you can visit the price comparison website which has been set up purely to compare the cost of ordering groceries from Tesco, Asda, Ocado and Sainsbury's for home delivery. By entering the details of the items you want to buy into www.mysupermarket.co.uk, you can find out which supermarket is cheaper and place your order straight away through the relevant supermarket website.

General Shopping

Before you invest in an expensive electrical or household item, such as a flat-screen television, washing machine or even a new bathroom, it is really worth comparing prices online. A two-minute search on a price comparison site for a 42 in plasma television shows exactly the same item priced between £800 and £1,299 at rival retailers. Simply choosing to buy from the cheapest outlet could save you £500.

Clothes Shopping

Comparing the cost of unbranded clothes and jewellery is less straightforward as many retailers stock different items, but the sites will still show a wide range of goods available from online and high street stores. The golden rule of price comparison sites still applies here, however. Your chances of bagging a bargain increase if you visit a couple of sites, as many will work with different retailers, and if you have time visit a couple of retailers' own sites too as there may be special offers or discount deals not available elsewhere.

The Websites

A range of well-known general retail price comparison websites include:

- **www.kelkoo.co.uk**: One of the biggest shopping comparison sites covering some 3,000 brands, Kelkoo includes items from online retailers such as Amazon.com as well as high street retailers including Comet, Dixons, John Lewis, WHSmith and Tesco. The site, which is owned by Yahoo! receives a commission every time you click through to a participating retailer's website.

- **www.shopping.com**: Another major price comparison site which is owned by eBay. The site lets you compare prices for all sorts of household, electrical and domestic items as well as toys, clothes, jewellery and books.

- **www.dealtime.co.uk**: This compares the cost of most electrical, household and personal items including video games, mobile phones and wine.

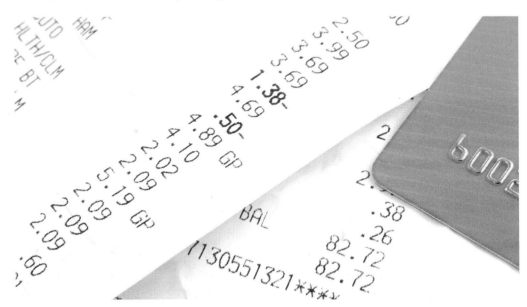

- **www.pricerunner.co.uk**: This offers customer reviews as well as price comparison tools for electrical, household and personal items including sunglasses, golf shoes and garden furniture

- **www.pricegrabber.co.uk**: PriceGrabber's wide-ranging comparison tools include clothing, consumer electronics, goods for babies and kids, sporting goods and musical instruments.

Travel

Holidays have been revolutionized by price comparison websites. The days of trailing around travel agents to choose the best holiday are long gone. Instead a range of sites allow you to compare the cost of flights and accommodation, or both, within minutes and from the comfort of your sofa.

Different Types of Websites

It is worthwhile checking a couple of sites before plumping for you holiday, not least because there are two main types of site:

- **Screenscrapers**: Many travel sites, including www.travelsupermarket.com and www.kayak.co.uk use screenscraper technology, which sends your details and requirements to many other websites and then reports back on the prices they quote. But also bear in mind that some airlines, such as Ryanair, are clamping down on screenscraper sites that do not direct customers to the airline site to buy the ticket but instead organize the purchase through their own website. Ryanair has begun to reject such tickets, so if you use a screenscraper site make sure it then directs you through to the airline site before you book – sites such as skyscanner (see the list below) do this.

- **Brokers**: But some other sites, such as www.expedia.co.uk and www.opodo.co.uk, operate as 'brokers', so while giving you the prices of other firms and suppliers, they also form direct relationships with some suppliers, allowing them to offer special deals not available anywhere else. However, many screenscraper sites also trawl these broker sites.

The Websites

There are an abundance of travel websites to choose from – here is a selection:

 www.cheapflights.co.uk: This publishes exclusive flight deals from hundreds of airlines, budget airlines and travel operators including Opodo and Expedia as well as specialist travel agencies.

- **www.ebookers.com**: This compares prices from 250 airlines and 86,000 hotels worldwide.

- **www.expedia.co.uk**: Expedia covers flights, hotel, car hire and holiday comparisons for more than 450 airlines and four million rooms worldwide.

- **www.kayak.co.uk**: This searches hundreds of travel sites, including online travel agencies, to compare prices for hotels, flights and car hire.

- **www.lastminute.com**: This well-known site lists cheap travel deals including flights, hotels or both – and by no means just 'last-minute' ones.

- **www.lowcostbeds.com**: This site compares hotel prices worldwide and offers a price guarantee so if a traveller finds the same hotel accommodation cheaper elsewhere, the site will match the price. It also compares flights – for 30 airlines – and car hire.

- **www.opodo.co.uk**: This 'flight broker' site, which is owned by nine of Europe's biggest airlines, offers comparisons on flights from 500 airlines, rooms at 65,000 hotels and 7,000 car rental locations.

- **www.priceline.co.uk**: This compares the cost of flights, hotels and car hire, but also enables travellers to decide how much (or little) they want to pay, allowing them to make their own offer of payment which will be accepted or declined within a minute.

- **www.skyscanner.net**: Skyscanner specializes in price comparison for flights.

- **www.travelocity.co.uk**: Travelocity gives holiday and flight comparisons.

- **www.travelsupermarket.com**: A sister site to moneysupermarket.com, this compares the cost of hotels, flights and car hire.

Specialist Websites

For people looking for great deals on, say, books, DVDs, CDs, computer games or mobile phones, there are a number of sites solely dedicated to each item. The advantage of this is that there is likely to be a wider range of that product available, thus making it easier to find exactly what you want without being distracted by other products on the site. There is also less chance of being provided with results for your particular search that include rogue items that have slipped through the search filter.

Downsides

Very specialist websites are often smaller outfits, which come with a couple of potential disadvantages:

✓ **Limited retailers**: Smaller sites *may* have a limited number of retailers providing prices to them. It is therefore possible that there may be better prices available which aren't included on the site.

✓ **Slower**: You may have to be more patient too as some sites may not be as easy to navigate as their bigger counterparts since they have not had as much money spent on their creation as the big names in the market.

Websites

But if you are searching for a book or mobile phone, for example, these sites will be worth a visit. Here are some of the specialist websites out there:

✓ **Books**: www.bookbrain.co.uk compares prices from the best online bookstores, while www.bookfinder4u.co.uk compares prices from 85 bookstores; www.addall.com compares from 41 online bookstores.

✓ **Mobile phones and tariffs**: www.onecompare.com, www.larilliam.co.uk and www.mobiles4everyone.com all specialize in mobile phone prices.

☑️ **Wine:** www.wine-searcher.com lists the current prices of wines and stockists.

☑️ **Cameras:** www.camerapricebuster.co.uk is indeed specialist, finding 'the UK's cheapest prices for Canon and Nikon Digital SLRs, lenses, accessories and memory cards.'

☑️ **Betting:** www.oddschecker.com compares the odds available at various high street and online betting shops.

☑️ **Shoes:** www.alltheshoes.co.uk claims to reveal the 'Best UK prices for Crocs, Birkenstocks, FitFlops, Havaianas, Merrell, Adidas, Nike and more ...'.

☑️ **Cigarettes:** www.netresort.co.uk is a good option for those who have no plans to kick the habit just yet...

☑️ **Petrol:** www.petrolprices.com has petrol prices for over 10,000 stations and receives approximately 8,000 daily updates.

Discounts
& General
Shopping

Vouchers and Coupons

Money-off and discount coupons are a popular way for manufacturers to entice consumers into trying new, existing, upgraded or rebranded products. Before filing coupons away in a drawer, be sure to check their expiry date as many need to be redeemed in a relatively short space of time.

Magazines and Newspapers

It is hard to flick through a magazine or paper without finding a discount coupon, either printed on the page or as a lose insert.

Action

If a coupon is on the page, cut it out immediately as you might not remember to go back to it.

Just in Case

Hang on to coupons for products you are unlikely to buy, as well as those you are, since some supermarkets and other retailers accept them if and deduct the value from the bill even if you haven't bought the item. Ask at the checkout or customer service desk what the store's policy is on such coupons.

Saturday Savings

Weekend newspapers are a particularly rich source of coupons, which may need to be redeemed within a week or even on the day, so buy your paper early and head to the shops to ensure you do not miss out.

Keep an Eye on Use-By Dates

As a general rule, vouchers printed in weekly magazines usually need to be used within a week, and those in monthly publications within a month, before the next issues go on sale.

Online Vouchers and Coupons

Never buy online without checking whether you can get a further discount with a coupon or money-off code from the retailer itself or a dedicated site. Hundreds of retailers supply these codes or coupons in order to attract new customers, or to direct them towards certain lines they want to shift. Discounts generally range from five per cent to 75 per cent, or may mean money off when customers spend over a certain amount, free delivery – generally on lower priced goods – or free returns, which will save you money on postage if you decide not to keep the products. Most discounts are aimed at online buyers, though some can be used in-store. You can find such discounts on virtually every type of product, from clothing, food and gifts through to electrical goods, housewares, holidays and perfumes.

Research

Using a search engine such as Google, type in the name of the retailer followed by the word 'discount'. Trawl through the list of results to find a code to be entered on the checkout page when completing your order.

Websites

Alternatively, try a website which does the work for you, listing alphabetically all the companies which supply these codes or coupons. The following are worth a visit:

 www.myvouchercodes.co.uk
 www.vouchercodes.com
 www.myukdiscountcodes.com
 www.couponsurfers.co.uk
 www.sendmediscounts.co.uk

Know Your Stuff

Most vouchers and codes have an expiry date, so use them quickly. Also, not all voucher codes are recognized, so you might need to work your way down a list, until you find one that works. Some sites give customers the opportunity to email feedback or reviews on whether they have been successful in using voucher codes, so it is helpful to read these.

Try, and Then Try Again

Sites are updated daily, so if you fail to find a promotional code for a particular product, have a look again the next day.

Where to Get Them

Retailers are too numerous to mention, but Dixons, Boden, Asda, Interflora, Dell and Marks & Spencer are among the well-known names which frequently offer these discounts.

Be the First to Know

Sign up for email alerts which will inform you when new vouchers and promotional codes become available.

Junk Mail

Many companies target potential new customers through unsolicited or junk mail, so scan it quickly before you consign it to the recycling bin – and you might be pleasantly surprised.

A Whole Range of Products

Insurance, travel, mobile phone and double-glazing companies send out a lot of promotional literature offering discounts, so look out for relevant offers if you are considering buying these goods.

Free Samples

This is a popular way to introduce new products, in particular laundry and food items, so you might be treated to a free sample as well as a discount voucher off your next purchase.

Future Planning

Hang on to voucher booklets which offer deals on a variety of different products. Even if they are not relevant now, they will come in handy when, for example, you need to renew car or household insurance.

Online Newsletters

When buying in-store or on the net, take up any offers to subscribe to an online newsletter and you may be rewarded with vouchers or advance information on sales.

Loyalty

As a reward for their loyalty, online subscribers often get preferential treatment over other customers, in the form of discounts on certain items or details of sale previews.

Some Examples

These newsletters are becoming an increasingly popular way for retailers to communicate with individual customers. Dorothy Perkins, Borders and Argos are just three of the many hundreds of companies offering this service.

Ask and Tick

You may need to be proactive about subscribing, so when purchasing an item in-store, ask whether the retailer sends out e-newsletters to customers. When buying online, you will normally be asked to tick a box if you wish to subscribe.

Cashback

It may sound too good to be true, but you really can get cashback on your purchases if you do your homework and sign up to the right website or card. The way it works is that when you buy an item online from a registered retailer via one of these websites, your account will be credited with either a percentage of the purchase price, or a fixed sum, which can be paid into your bank account or by cheque. Or, if you use a card, use it to pay for goods and services and earn a small percentage on every transaction.

Cashback Websites

A huge range of products can be bought via cashback websites, and Marks & Spencer, Next, The White Company, Sky, Marriott Hotels, BT and Egg are amongst the many participating companies.

Do Not Be Blinded

You will only make savings if you have already found the best deal via a comparison website. You will not be getting a bargain if you are lured by the prospect of earning cash into paying more in the first place. For example, a five per cent discount on a £300 camera will save you £15 – but this will be a false economy if Amazon is selling it for £250.

Choices

Carry out a search for companies offering cashback, or visit one of the following sites:

 www.quidco.com
 www.wepromiseto.co.uk
 www.topcashback.co.uk
 www.rpoints.com

Check the Small Print

The largest percentage of cash does not necessarily mean the best site, as some sites keep the first £5 of earnings and only pay out over that amount.

Check the Threshold

Some sites only pay out once you have reached a threshold, so unless you are planning major purchases, opt for one that will pay out every time you make a purchase.

Eggs in More Than One Basket

Join more than one site to maximize cashback if you are likely to use them a lot.

Patience

Sites can be slow to pay out, so it is wise not to spend the money before you have received it.

Cashback With Your Credit Card

Cashback on the high street is very limited as present, but register your credit or debit card with www.greasypalm.co.uk to earn cash when using the card in stores including House of Fraser and Superdrug.

Cashback Cards

These are normal credit cards with a difference – a percentage of everything you buy is paid back to you. This is generally around one per cent, but can occasionally be higher. Not all cards are accepted everywhere, however.

Best Cards

The Egg Money Card and Barclycard's Cashback card are two of the best, though payouts are capped above a certain level.

Must-Do Rule

Only use these cards if you pay your balance off in full every month, otherwise any potential gains will be completely wiped out by the interest charged.

Loyalty Cards

Various stores and companies encourage customers to opt for loyalty card schemes, on which they collect points with every purchase. These points can be redeemed in the store, online or on various other goods and services.

Schemes

Tesco's Clubcard

With the Clubcard, customers are paid one point per pound, and each point earns a penny discount off shopping at Tesco.

- **Partners**: The card can also be used to earn points when spending at Johnson Cleaners, EON, Marriott and a few other companies.

- **Vouchers**: Points vouchers are sent out quarterly, together with coupons giving further discounts (usually in the form of points) on items customers buy frequently.

- **Bigger deals**: Make vouchers go further by redeeming them on Clubcard deals, where they will be worth four times as much. You can make savings on days out, magazine subscriptions and restaurants, for example.

- **Promotions**: Look out for in-store or online promotions which offer additional Clubcard points.

- **Find out more**: For further information, log on to www.tesco.com.

Boots Advantage Card

The Advantage card is the most generous loyalty scheme, as customers earn four points, worth 4p, for every pound spent when shopping in a store or on the company's website, www.boots.com. When shopping in-store, insert your Advantage card into a card reader machine to print off vouchers which are redeemable on your purchases.

Health club: Advantage cardholders who sign up to Boots Health Club will receive discount and double points vouchers on a regular basis.

Double your money: Boots frequently hosts double or triple points days, where customers will earn points giving them as much as a 12 per cent discount on purchases.

Nectar

Nectar cards can be used to earn points when spending in Sainsbury's, BP petrol stations, Dollond & Aitchinson and others. You usually earn two points for every pound spent, and points are worth just over 0.5p each.

Extra: You can earn further points by participating in online surveys or joining up, as a new customer, to Nectar partners, including the AA.

Treats: Points can be redeemed in your host store (usually Sainsbury's) or online at the Nectar website www.nectar.com for treats, days out and purchases.

Airmiles

These are collected in a variety of ways, including shopping at various stores such as www.play.com and Homebase or purchasing Lloyds TSB financial products. Airmiles are worth around 7p each, and can be used for tickets to attractions, days out and car hire, for example.

More

Waterstone's and Morrisons also run schemes. It is always worth asking if such a scheme exists.

Store Cards

Store cards are very similar to credit cards in that you can spend up to a set credit limit and have the option to pay the balance off in full or only pay the monthly minimum. Many stores give discounts and other preferential treatment to new and existing account customers. Beware that interest rates can be high, so you will only gain if you pay the balance off in full each month. See also the Clothes & Accessories chapter (page 144).

Benefits

The best savings are usually reserved for new customers, in the form of a percentage discount on their first purchase.

Discount on Signing Up

Depending on where you shop, the initial discount may be as much as 10 or 15 per cent, though you may need to spend more than a certain amount – possibly £50 or £100 – before becoming eligible. Introductory offers include the likes of a 10 per cent discount at Debenhams, both in-store and online, and a five per cent saving when you spend over £50 at Bhs. Rather than wasting a discount on a small purchase, wait until you are updating your wardrobe or club together with friends so that you can make substantial savings.

Preview Evenings

Other benefits include sale preview evenings for account customers, where you will be given the opportunity to shop at sale prices before the general public is allowed in.

Credit Cards as 'Store Cards'

American Express customers who are enrolled on the company's Membership Rewards scheme are entitled to a massive 30 per cent discount when using their card in a Gap store on certain dates, or a 10 per cent saving in branches of Harvey Nichols at various times.

Catalogues and Online Stores

Customers ordering from a catalogue for the first time can be well-rewarded for their efforts. Discounts are usually in the form of a percentage or fixed sum off the initial purchase. See also the Clothes & Accessories chapter (page 144). And it's no secret that buying online usually trumps buying in-store for price.

Catalogues

Buying from a catalogue is often not the cheapest way to shop, so, if you are after a specific, branded product, do your maths before you order.

Price Comparisons

Visit price comparison websites to find out where the item can be bought most cheaply and only order from the catalogue when you are satisfied that, once the discount has been applied, you will be paying less than the lowest price you have found elsewhere.

Do Not Be Tempted

You will usually be given the option to take out a credit account and pay in instalments but rates of interest are high and you will only make savings if you pay for the item in one go.

Big Players

The major players in the home shopping catalogue league are Littlewoods, Freemans, Grattan and Next. Each of these companies provides generous discounts on first orders, though these change from time to time.

- **Littlewoods:** Gives new customers £15 off when they spend £25.

- **Freemans and Grattan:** Give a 20 per cent discount off first orders.

- **Next:** Existing customers are rewarded for their loyalty to Next, as twice a year they have the opportunity to save 15 per cent if they order from preview catalogues before a specified date.

- **Boden:** This is one of a number of companies that gives discounts of up to 20 per cent to new and existing catalogue customers.

Online Catalogues

Even if you prefer to shop from a printed catalogue rather than the online version, check out the company's website on a regular basis for updates on sales and special, discounted purchases.

Online Stores

Internet stores can afford to keep their prices low as they do not have the same overheads as high street showrooms. Lower rents in out of town warehouses, no shop floor staff and an absence of eye-catching displays mean that they can afford to pass their savings on to customers. See also the Clothes & Accessories chapter (page 144).

Dedicated Online Stores

These are stand-alone retailers with no high street or retail park presence. They rely heavily on a combination of low prices and good customer service to attract and keep customers.

Some are highly specialized while others stock a huge selection of products, making them, in effect, online department stores.

Amazon (www.amazon.co.uk)

Amazon is the biggest and best known of the online-only department stores, and stocks millions of items, including books, electronics, toys, home and garden, sports, jewellery and beauty products.

 Delivery: This is free when you spend over £15, so combine small purchases to save on postage.

Updates: Customers receive regular email alerts, informing them of sales and even better deals on already low prices.

Amazon bargains: Log on to www.pricecutreview.com/uk to find current bargains from Amazon, which are being sold at half the original price or less.

Other Online-Only Retailers

Amazon seems to almost have a monopoly on the generalized, departmentstore-like content (though eBay is rapidly becoming one), but there are many other more specialized online-only retailers that will have deals and discounts sections or offers on their websites, such as Play.com and ASOS.

Online Versions of High Street Stores

Most chains and many independent stores now sell online too, but customers should not be misled into thinking that prices and stock are always the same. Lower overheads mean that many stores offer lower prices on items sold online rather than in-store.

Compare prices: Before buying in a store, check whether the price is lower online.

✅ **Delivery**: Find out whether there is a charge for delivery and whether returns are free if you change your mind, as these costs will affect where you eventually make your purchase. When ordering large or heavy items, choose a retailer that provides a free delivery service, otherwise you may have to factor the cost of hiring a van into your budget.

✅ **Haggle**: If you prefer to buy in store – perhaps because you want the product immediately – ask if a lower, online price can be matched.

✅ **Collect**: To save the hassle of queuing, waiting and delivery charges, find out if you can order the item online and collect it in store. Argos and PC World are two retailers offering this service, enabling you to pick up your order at a time that suits you, rather than waiting in for hours for a delivery.

Haggling

Haggling – or negotiating for a better price – has moved out of the marketplace and into even the smartest stores. Many of us may not be used to such an upfront approach, but get it right and it can be very rewarding. In the current financial climate, with shoppers staying away and profits squeezed, some retailers are only too happy to accept a lower price rather than lose a sale.

In-Store – Do Your Homework

Checking out competitors' prices before asking for a discount will put you in a far better bargaining position. Also, find out on what day of the week the stores needs to meet its sales targets – and shop the day before.

Speak to the Manager

Rather than dealing with a junior assistant, ask to speak to the manager who will have the authority to be flexible on price. Managers are trained to deal with all manner of customer queries, so there is no need to worry about being thought of as cheap or mean. Let the manager know if there is competition in pricing from a rival store.

Control Your Demeanour

Be calm and reasonable as you are far more likely to get a discount than if you lose your temper.

Be Flexible

Rather than lowering the price, the store may be prepared to include more items, such as free software or a printer when a customer is buying a computer.

Hard Cash

Offer cash if possible as nothing beats it.

On the Shelf

You are more likely to succeed when buying items which have been in stock for a while, rather than brand new or recently upgraded lines which are selling well.

Haggling Online

Visit www.jalebi.co.uk, a new, fast-growing buying community which aims to get people together to buy products at the prices they want.

Jalebi

Jalebi draws on the power of collective buying to enable people to obtain maximum discounts resulting from what is effectively a bulk buy. The site currently focuses on electrical items, travel, home and contents insurance, but has plans to extend the range of products and services. This is how it works:

- **Post:** A member places a posting on the site, with details of the product of interest – for example, a television.

- **'Shop':** Other members then look at the posting, decide if they would like to buy the same television and register their interest.

- **Group:** Once a group has formed, a member is then in a position to go to a local retailer, saying that there is a group of people who want the same product, and negotiate a discount.

Online Auctions

Online auctions are an incredibly popular way of shopping, with great prices on brand new, everyday items, plus collectibles, antiques, one-offs and, of course, cars. eBay is the biggest and best-known, but police and government auction sites offer great bargains, too. See also the Clothes & Accessories chapter (pages 144–171) for further advice.

Shopping on eBay

If you are new to eBay, take time to navigate the site and get to know the way it works in order to get the best possible prices and protect yourself from being ripped off.

Getting Started

Start by registering on the site – you will need to provide a credit card number for verification as well as personal details. You will also need to chose a username, which will be your identity on eBay – for additional privacy, select one which is different from your email address.

Searching

Once registered, you are free to browse, or do a specific search by typing what you are looking for in the search box. Try to be as specific as possible – for example, type in 'Sony digital 32 inch TV' rather than simply 'Sony TV' – to avoid having to trawl through hundreds of results.

Be Careful

Review the items you are interested in as well as the sellers very thoroughly:

 Description: Look at photos and read descriptions carefully, particularly if you are buying an item that is second-hand, as quality varies enormously.

 **Postage**: Most sellers include the postage costs, which the buyer is liable to pay, so bear these in mind to ensure you are getting a true bargain.

Returns: You are buying unseen (in the flesh), so check whether there is a returns policy.

Seller: Check the seller's reputation by clicking on the feedback rating. Read what other buyers have said about the seller's reliability, product quality and level of service. Only choose a seller with a rating of 98 per cent or above and who has been trading for at least 90 days.

Bidding

Once you have found an item you want and a seller you have confidence in, you are finally ready to bid. An online auction works in the same way as a standard auction carried out in an auction house, in that the highest bid wins and, once accepted, cannot be withdrawn. Open the auction page of the item and enter the amount you want to bid, then confirm this bid after ensuring that your bid is higher than the current one. If you are later outbid, eBay will send an email notification and give you the chance to place a new bid. Auctions have a cut-off date and time, and you will be informed by email if your bid is successful.

Buy It Now

If you see a 'buy it now' listing, you will be able to buy the item instantly at the stated price, without needing to bid for it.

Payment

Some sellers ask to be paid by debit, credit card, or cheque, though eBay's preferred payment method is via Paypal, which transfers funds between buyers and sellers so they do not have to exchange bank details.

Receipt

When the item arrives, check it carefully to ensure it matches the description and is in good condition, then leave positive feedback on the seller if the transaction went well.

Buying Tactic

You will generally pay lower prices when bidding for out of season goods which are less popular, so plan ahead and look for garden furniture in December and Christmas trees in July.

Police and Government Auctions

The credit squeeze means that you are increasingly likely to find brand new items from companies that have gone into liquidation as well as government surplus and items seized in police and customs raids for sale in online auctions.

Police

Visit www.bumblebeeauctions.co.uk to bid for items classified as police property. These include possessions recovered from the proceeds of crime, lost property and items seized by bailiffs. As well as knock-down prices, you can also be assured that the seller is a safe bet!

Government

For information on government auctions nationwide, subscribe to Government Auction news at www.ganews.co.uk.

TV Shopping Channels

Despite their name, many people prefer to shop online when buying from a TV discount shopping channel. The main ones are sister channels BidTV and Price-drop TV, which both operate falling price auctions and claim to sell 'quality products at bargain prices'. You will need to register before you can bid.

Falling Price Auctions

As the name suggests, the price actually falls during the course of the auction, but, unlike on eBay, large quantities are for sale, rather than a single item. Some items are well-known brands whereas others are unbranded. Prices can drop to as low as £1 for electrical and other items, so there are huge bargains to be had.

Buy Now or Bid

To secure an item, purchasers can choose to 'buy now', wait for the auction to close and only pay the lower, closing price. Alternatively, buyers can choose to place a bid and will get the product if it falls to that price or less. When a TV product is being sold live on TV you can buy it instantly through the website. If the TV product you are interested in has yet to go on air, you can enter a bid in advance on the website.

Avoid Charges

Buying online means you avoid high call charges, which are payable even if you are unsuccessful in your bid. Also, watch out for high delivery charges – make sure you know these in advance of making a bid or an item may not turn out to be such a bargain after all.

Discount Stores, Factory Outlets & Shopping Villages

A flurry of discount stores have sprung up in town centres and out-of-town retail parks. Product ranges may differ but what they all have in common is low prices, no-frills, high volume and quick turnaround sales. See also the chapter on Clothes & Accessories (pages 144–171) for more in-depth detail on the shops covered here.

Big Names in Discount Stores

Makro, Costco, TK Maxx, Primark, Matalan, Poundland, Wilkinson, Netto, Aldi and Lidl are the biggest companies in this sector.

Makro

Makro has 33 cash-and-carry warehouses throughout the UK, specializing in food, catering and office supplies. It is aimed at trade and business customers, so not everyone is eligible to shop here.

Costco

Costco sells a vast range of goods, including food, drink, electrical items, furniture and sports items. Like Makro, only trade customers can buy at its 20 warehouses throughout the UK.

TK Maxx

TK Maxx stocks remaindered, returned and end-of-line clothes, accessories, sportswear, toys and homewares, from designers and big brands. Discounts of up to 60 per cent are offered.

Primark

Primark is arguably the cheapest of the lot and steadfastly refuses to pay for music in its stores so savings can be passed down to customers. It specializes in fashion, but the selection of homewares is gradually increasing.

Matalan

Matalan is famed for stylish own-label fashion and homewares at rock bottom prices. Soft furnishings and interior accessories are right on trend, but at a fraction of the price paid for similar items in fashionable stores.

Poundland

Poundland stocks thousands of homewares, toys, DIY, food, health and beauty, and baby products (and more), all priced at £1. Look out for deals of the week.

Wilkinson

Wilkinson has a huge choice of branded and own-brand housewares, DIY accessories, stationery, health and beauty products and a whole lot more. It has a very comprehensive website with an even bigger product range.

Netto, Aldi and Lidl

These are essentially discount supermarkets, selling a mix of market leading brands and more obscure labels. Take your own bags as you may be charged for them.

Factory Shops

Many manufacturers and retailers have permanent factory shops, which sell a mixture of old stock, returned orders, discontinued lines, damaged goods, seconds and ex-display stock at discounts of up to 70 per cent off the original retail price.

Find Out Where They Are

Ask whether the company has a factory shop, as many do not advertise the fact. Some factory shops form part of shopping villages, while others are stand-alone stores.

Is It Worth It?

You may need to travel a long way to the store, so you will need to offset savings against the cost in petrol.

Shopping Villages

More than 40 shopping villages are scattered round the UK, containing a selection of stores selling brand names at low prices. Fashion, homewares, sportswear and toys are just some of the sectors represented, at discounts of up to 70 per cent.

Benefits

As well as low prices, parking is free and this is a convenient way to shop, with many brands under one roof, in a stylish retail environment.

Big Players

McArthur Glen – which has seven outlets – and Bicester Shopping Village are among the largest shopping villages.

Outlet Stores

A few of the famous names with outlet stores include John Lewis, The White Company, Monsoon, Jigsaw, Villeroy & Bosch, Burberry, Calvin Klein and Dior.

Be Quick

If you see something you like, snap it up fast as bargains do not hang around for long.

Designer Warehouse Sales

Unlike factory shops, which offer year-round discounts, some companies hold occasional warehouse sales in which they hope to shift a huge amount of discounted stock in the space of a few days. Expect savings of up to 80 per cent.

Sign Up for a Sale

Ask if the company holds such sales, and request to be put on a mailing list so you will be informed when the next one is taking place.

Examples

Ghost clothing and Designer's Guild both have regular, well-organised and well-stocked warehouse sales.

Online Information

Register with www.fashionconfidential.com for insider information on designer fashion and accessory warehouse and sample sales. Discounts at such sales are substantial but prices are still high, so be warned!

Sales and Other Discounts

There are all kinds of sales and reductions that happen at specific times in the year or a shop's programme. While some stores tip off customers well in advance, a little perseverance is needed in others, so ask shop assistants or the manager when the sale will be taking place. The more you look, the more you will find a plethora of other ways of chipping away at the prices of products you wish to buy.

Seasonal Sales

With so many other money-saving ways to shop, you could be forgiven for neglecting seasonal sales, traditionally held mid-summer and right after Christmas.

Shop Early

It goes without saying that you should be prepared to get there early to snap up the best bargains.

Shop Online

Some store sales – for example Next's – start online at the same time as in-store, so you can shop from the comfort of your armchair without missing out on bargains.

Ex-Display

Stores are often keen to get rid of ex-display items so that they can make room for new items.

Negotiate

It is worth asking for a hefty discount on such items, particularly if they are not part of the usual stock – such as cushions and furniture used in the window display of a fashion chain.

Check Before You Buy

Such items are usually sold 'as seen', so examine carefully and point any damage out to the store manager.

Buy One, Get One Free (BOGOF)

Commonly referred to by the delightful acronym BOGOF, this type of offer gives a discount of 50 per cent, as you are literally getting two items for the price of one. Look out, too, for similar three-for-the-price-of-two offers, with savings of a third.

Where to Find It

Most commonly found in supermarkets but you will occasionally find these offers in other retailers, including Boots and DIY sheds.

Beware False Economies

Take care when buying items with a relatively short shelf life – in particular food – as they will not be bargains if they have reached their use-by dates before you are ready to use them.

Employee or Union Discounts

If you work for a large organisation or are a member of a union, ask your manager or union representative whether any discounts are available on group memberships or company products.

Typical Savings

In addition to company products, the most common savings are on gym memberships, health and dental insurance, and interest-free loans on travel to work.

Buy from Abroad

Do some research before you travel overseas to find out which products are worth buying while you are away. The strong Euro has all but wiped out the substantial savings on food and wine purchased in France, but if you look carefully, you can still buy for less than you would pay in the UK.

What to Buy

As a general rule, buy products in their country of origin. On the continent, look out for Le Creuset pans in France, olive oil from Italy and Mango clothing in Spain.

The United States

The US still offers good value for DVDs, cameras and games, but check that items are compatible with UK systems.

Beware of Tax

Duty is payable on all items over £145 purchased outside the UK, so this will cut heavily into any savings.

Refer a Friend

Recommending friends and family members as new customers can be lucrative as some companies offer incentives for doing so. Boden will credit existing accounts with £2.50 off the next purchase for each name supplied, while Standard Life Health Insurance offers Marks & Spencer vouchers.

Discounts Targeted at Specific Groups

Age and status can have the advantage of earning you further discounts on a wide variety of products and services.

Students

Deals on shopping, entertainment, eating out and travel are available to students – for further information visit www.studentdiscounts.co.uk.

Over 60s

Focus Do It All and Wyevale Garden centres are just two of the stores offering 10 per cent discounts to customers aged over 60.

Late Deals

If you can afford to be flexible with your time and leave making plans right up until the last minute, you may be able to make substantial savings on the price of theatre tickets, shows and holidays.

Online

Visit www.lastminute.com to check out what is available at short notice. More specialist websites include www.lastminutetravel.com and www.lastminutetheatretickets.com – and many other websites offer late deals in addition to their standard deals.

Telephone

Contact the relevant theatre on the day of the performance for good deals on standby and cancelled tickets.

Online Guides

Log on to an online guide to find dozens of places to shop for less. Two of the best for home and garden bargains are www.homesandbargains.co.uk and www.gooddealdirectory.co.uk, which also features discount fashion. And sign up with www.moneysavingexpert.com for weekly newsletters on where to get the best deals and how to make the most significant savings.

Food Shopping

Supermarkets

As inflation reaches its 16-year high in the UK, consumers are looking for savings wherever they can get them, especially as the rising cost of living has been estimated at 21 per cent more in 2008 than in the first half of 2007. Of course, supermarkets are also feeling the pinch: transportation and wholesale/supplier costs have risen too, which has forced up the price of nearly everything. In a bid to win and woo cash-strapped customers, the supermarkets are all promising to help us beat inflation. There is now a price war on, and the stores are making a big deal out of their big deals. But how do you know if their headline offers, deals and price cuts really could save you money?

Supermarket Sweeps

Prices are being slashed across the top five leading supermarkets in the UK. Two of them – Asda and Tesco – went head-to-head in a milk skirmish, with one store cutting the price of a two-pint (one litre) bottle to 50p while stocks lasted. While their fight to get footfall through their sliding doors rages on, it's worth getting in quick to grab a deal. Here's how to make the best out of a price war:

Freezing

Is the foodstuff at the centre of the battle freezable? If so, it's worth buying extra while stocks last.

Saving Over Time

Is it something that you need regularly? If so, it's worth going a little further to save those extra pennies.

Loyalty Card Points in Sales

Can you redeem Clubcard points against them? There's a double bargain in this move if you can bag a special offer and use your Clubcard to pay for it.

Case Study: Keeping the Coupons!

You can always save on your shopping bill, and everyone around the world is looking for the best bargains. One man, who divides his time living between the UK and Canada, speaks about living on a budget and trying to beat inflation: 'We are on a fixed income like most of the real world and always on the lookout for deals. I am always pitting one company against another to get a better deal on insurance, cable, phone, etc. You have to do it. I know you are thinking: "I just do not have the time". But believe me, it all adds up quickly so take the time and do some comparison shopping – after all, it is your money.

'The cost of fuel for the car is up so everything else has risen while our income shrinks. So I hunt for bargains. For example, I just went over to Shoppers DrugMart today and found some WeightWatchers cookies on for half price and I happened to have eight coupons for 50 cents off each box in my wallet. I had to walk home about a mile to get them but it was worth it. Hey that was $4.00 I just saved as we buy them all the time.

'We shop at Shop and Save or any of the Loblaws Chain as we have our bank accounts there and so have no monthly bank charges. It is another way to save our hard-earned money. We collect store points on purchases at one store, and if we use the store's environmentally friendly cloth bags at the check out, we receive bonus points for each dollar we spend. So we do not get any more plastic bags as well so it is a win-win for the environment and us – in the course of a year we can get between $100 and $200 dollars a year in free groceries.

'When I see coupons that we use, I always take a lot of them as the expiry usually lasts for a while. It is money in the bank in the long run. We also collect Airmiles both with another store card and our Amex card. With this, we have gotten free stuff such as printers, cameras, both digital and SLR, iPods, tools, suitcases and free trips during the past 18 months, which helps us as our families live in the UK and we spend a lot of months in Europe. So I reckon because of a little extra time spent comparison shopping, collecting coupons and Airmiles, we can afford the extras now and then without feeling guilty.'

Look Around

Who has the largest amount of best price deals? It may not be your usual shop – so be prepared to hunt in a new field.

Customer Comment: Shopping Around Does Work

Jenny, mum-of-three from Brixton, UK, says: 'For all their purchasing power the supermarkets are still ripping customers off. The answer to "Rip-Off Britain" is to shop around. As a family of five we have reduced our outgoings by 40 per cent over the past 12 months.'

Be Circumspect

Not all the prices in the stores are being cut; some are being raised, and there's wisdom in the saying 'too good to be true'. Sales can sometimes result in food you don't want, need or use being grabbed in the bargain frenzy.

Customer Comment: False Economies

Jeremy Main from Surrey, UK says: 'Stores should lower the price of all food and not give false incentives. For example, why do you have to spend £50 before you get a discount on fuel? This is no good if you don't spend that much.'

Sudden Price Hikes

With the 'milk war', for example, there are ethical issues at stake in that UK dairy farmers are being hit hard by these price cuts, resulting in some strike action – which often has the effect of forcing up the price suddenly.

Customer Comment: Be Aware

Adam Knight from Mitcham, UK, says: 'Stores may be starting price wars on certain items but they are simply raising the price of other products to offset the difference.'

Reduced to Clear

Most leading supermarkets will proffer a range of heavily-discounted foodstuffs which are approaching their end-of-shelf life. It is worth taking the time to find out what individual stores do with their sell-by goods: some of them price it down and put it out for purchase; others may simply throw it away. It's also worth being cheeky and asking (politely) for a discount on damaged goods.

'Sell By', 'Best Before' and 'Use By'

'Sell by' and 'best before' dates do not mean the same as 'use by'. A use-by date really means it's the end of a product's life, for example, eggs, milk or meat produce. A best-before date is a guideline; sometimes foodstuff is good a day or two after the best-before date. A sell-by date is an arbitrary measure telling staff when to replenish stock on the shelves, but the food may be good for a week or so yet.

Where to Find

Here are just a few examples of where you can find best-buy prices on reduced to clear goods:

- **In-store bakery items**: Supermarkets promise that their bakery goods are fresh each day. Late at night, they will often bag up items at knock-down prices which, although still fresh and will last a few days, must be sold to make way for freshly-baked goods each day.

- **Meat and fish**: If you intend to eat, or freeze, the fresh meat or fish, then it's worth looking for meat at discount prices; don't try this if you don't intend to cook or freeze it on the day of purchase however!

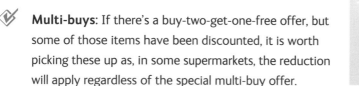

Shop-damaged goods: Dented tins, multi-packs of crisps, individually wrapped chocolate biscuits and other such items may have been dropped, ripped or opened accidentally in-store, which has necessitated the reduction, but the contents may be undamaged and well within the sell-by date

Last-one-in-the-shop: Some supermarkets will give you a discount on fruit or veg. For example, the author needed strawberries and there was just one pack left in the store. The assistant noticed that a couple of strawberries were verging on the undesirable, but as it was the last box in the store, the author requested a discount and bagged the lot for 50p (down from £1.50).

Multi-buys: If there's a buy-two-get-one-free offer, but some of those items have been discounted, it is worth picking these up as, in some supermarkets, the reduction will apply regardless of the special multi-buy offer.

Buy One, Get One Free (BOGOF)

These types of deals are great if you really need what's being offered. Some points to consider to maximize the usefulness of such bargains are:

Need

Just because it is a special deal, if it's not on your usual shopping list, don't buy it. However, if you know that a supermarket is advertising several of these three-for-the-price-of-two or Bogof offers for items you get regularly, such as bread, teabags or tissues, grab as much as you can, as this will reduce your shopping bill significantly.

Legal Issues

There have been investigations by the Advertising Standards Agency (ASA) about Bogof.

The price takes into account the fact that two items are being sold. The price of 'one' is somewhat nominal and has been found to have been raised when used as part of a BOGOF deal. While the cost per item is proportionately cheaper than if bought on its own, it is not actually half price, critics claim. So be canny about your purchases.

'25%' or '50% Extra Free'

The ASA is also investigating this sort of deal, following some customer letters which claimed that stores and manufacturers sometimes put up the price of a product before coming out with a short-term 25 per cent extra-free offer.

Brand Loyalty

You pay for the familiarity and comfort factor of buying a household name. A known label carries perhaps quality assurance, the patina of authority, or social standing. However, in many cases, there is no real difference in the quality or taste of a product between a brand name and the store's own label, except, perhaps, in the case of Heinz Baked Beans.

Read the Ingredients

The reason why most products from your local store taste similar to leading brands should become obvious from reading the list of ingredients. For example, Sainsbury's own brand chicken Korma and Be Good To Yourself Chicken Korma sauces have nearly the same ingredients list, in similar quantities, to that of Sharwood's Patak range, but for nearly half the price.

What's the Difference?

1 kg packets of McDougall's or Homepride self-raising flour in various shops were between 20 per cent to 30 per cent more expensive than the supermarkets' own brands – if anyone can tell the difference when it's mixed into a fruit cake, they deserve a gold medal.

Frosty Welcome

Big price savings can be made on frozen food. Local frozen food specialists often get a range of top brands for rock-bottom prices because they buy in bulk. But even then, their own brands may work out cheaper; for example, International brand Bird's Eye was retailing its 400 g bag of peas for almost double the amount (that's nearly 100 per cent) than the price of the same-sized bag of own-brand peas. Both sets of peas were small and green and tasted the same when cooked.

Own-Brand v. Own-Brand

There's often little difference between the quality of various supermarkets' own-brand goods either. For example, Tesco's Luxury Soft and Sainsbury's Super Soft four-pack toilet paper are much of a muchness, with no discernible difference in look or feel.

Down-Branding

Even within some stores, they have their own premier brand and their basics or no-frills range. Down-branding from the household names or the store's own 'premium' brands towards the no-frills range can knock between 15 per cent to 30 per cent off a family's annual shopping bill according to consumer champion websites www.mysupermarket.co.uk and www.moneysavingexpert.com.

Table: ITV1's Downshift Challenge

Money guru Martin Lewis made some startling discoveries in his ITV1 Tonight: Supermarket Cheap programme. By following a family that he had challenged to downshift from household names and premium brands, he found that the family could save up to 30 per cent without losing out on taste, quality or nutritional value. The following table gives an example of his findings:

Product	Mainstream brand	Supermarket own	Supermarket economy
Jaffa Cakes	£1.88	£1.15	£1.08
Tea bags (240 pk)	£2.99	£2.19	£0.87
Toilet roll	£1.81	£1.54	£0.40
Toothpaste	£1.76	£0.39	£0.31
Lager (4 x 500 ml cans)	£4.78	£2.19	£0.88

Source: Martin Lewis/ITV1 Tonight: Supermarket Cheap, 2008

Store Manager Comment: Changing Lanes

A local Sainsbury's store manager commented: 'People who like their brands have tended to fall into two categories: those who want quality and those who always shop on a budget. Quality-seekers will go to Waitrose or Marks & Spencer, while those who want budget will go to Iceland or Lidl. But recently we have seen more of the quality-seekers coming in to buy our own-branded food, perhaps because they are finding the purse strings a bit tighter at the moment. On the other end of the scale, people who have usually gone elsewhere for cheap goods are also coming in because the quality assurance of the Sainsbury's label gives them some confidence that what they are getting is good food and great service.'

Advertising

The shops are all telling us they can help us beat inflation. However, a supermarket's aim is not to help customers out of a tight spot, but to make us spend money in their stores. Beware of the following 'lures'.

TV Tactics

Ever since Marks & Spencer produced a TV advert using a silken-voiced woman declaring that 'this was not just any food', other supermarkets have muscled in. They are trying to lure buyers in by sounding genuine. Don't be fooled: they might sound convincing, but while they get you hooked on one product on TV, other items you will buy in-store may not be cheaper than the competition.

Public Punch-Ups

UK supermarkets are now adopting the tactic familiar to US TV advertising, where stores go to head in public to prove that they offer better value for money than each other. Recently, the ASA has forced one of the supermarkets to withdraw two of its adverts for a breach of standards. So when adverts tell you they offer the best prices, keep the following factors in mind:

Distance

If you have to drive further to get to the best price, are you spending more on petrol than you are saving?

Club Points

It may be worth taking advantage of being loyal to your store, rather than chasing short-term price cuts elsewhere. For example, Tesco claims to give you 1p back every time you use your Tesco card. Other stores give you three to four points per £1 you spend. If you use a club or points card regularly, how much have you saved on it? Is it worth switching stores now, or staying loyal and maximizing your points?

Check Everything

Each store claims to be cheaper – but how true is this? Prices change quicker than TV advertising – have a look yourself at www.mysupermarket.co.uk before you do your weekly shop.

Look Further

Don't just compare the one or two products the stores are advertising, but compare the price of everything you buy regularly. Item for item, what works out cheaper? Which store will give you the best prices across a range of goods?

Leaflets and Promotions

Money-off vouchers and special promotions are a great way to help you make the most of available bargains for your weekly shop.

Junk Mail

Don't throw away any marketing that comes through your door. There may be some discount coupons that could be useful for you or a family member. Keep them in your purse for when you go shopping.

Online Vouchers

Look online for money-off vouchers. Sometimes they are on sites such as www.mysupermarket.co.uk or they are on the store's own website. You can print these off and use them against certain items; beware, though: not all the vouchers may be for everyone to use. The same applies to discount delivery codes, which are internet codes that can cut the price of home shopping.

Get the Same Deal Another Time

Ask for what are commonly called 'raincheck' vouchers – if a special offer item is not in stock, the store manager might give you a voucher entitling you to the same deal at a later date.

Points Promotions

In-store deals offering extra points for a particular product is a great way to save for that rainy day or big celebration.

Free Samples Are Useful!

Don't throw away free samples. They are great to keep for a rainy day when you run out of teabags or to cut down one month on more expensive household items such as washing powder.

Surveys

If you are offered the chance to win free shopping for a year just by filling in a survey from your energy or car insurance company, then go for it. What have you got to lose? Free groceries for a year must be the best price ever!

Home Shopping

Save yourself from being misled by advertising. If you can't afford the time to explore the stores in person, there are websites you can use to check out where the best prices really are. By taking a few minutes to explore these, you may find that even the upper end of the market such as Waitrose, through its online delivery service Ocado, might just have a better deal on some top-quality goods than Tesco. But you wouldn't know unless you ignore the ads and go straight to the supermarket comparison sites to see for yourself.

mySupermarket

This website, www.mysupermarket.co.uk, allows you to do several things to help make your shopping an easier, less costly experience. It aims to: compare prices across four leading supermarkets, help you cut the calories in your shopping trolley and save money.

How to Use

Step 1: Fill your virtual trolley with your usual weekly purchases.

Step 2: Conduct a 'shopping trolley swap' with another supermarket on the site – this takes about 60 seconds, depending on how much is in your virtual trolley.

Step 3: See how much you could save by carrying out the swap – the site claims it could be 20 per cent each week – and place your order, ready for it to be delivered to you.

Loyalty Programme

mySupermarket has a loyalty scheme where you can gain i-points as well as the usual points you will get on your store loyalty or club card. These i-points can be traded at www.ipoints.co.uk for a variety of goods, days out or gift ideas.

At-a-Glance Best Prices

The site will show daily deals and best prices on a range of products at each supermarket. So, regardless of whether you want to swap supermarkets or not, you can see at a glance where the best prices are.

Fixture Ferrets

No, its not a home decorating service offered by wild rodents, but a cracking website which lets you know which supermarkets are offering discounts, Bogofs and special deals. It claims to enable you to save £10 or more off your monthly bills, which can mean a saving of £120 a year. It also features more supermarkets than mySupermarket, including Somerfield and Morrison's. Check out www.fixtureferrets.com.

Google it!

A quick search for 'best prices for food shopping in the UK' will throw up a host of websites, chat forums and even blogs which are quick to notice where the best price buys are. Have a look at sites such as:

- **www.bizrate.co.uk**: For best prices on wine, champagne, beer and spirits for party planning.

- **www.ciao.co.uk**: This also compares the price of brand name goods, such as Kellogg's cereals.

- **www.chowhound.com**: This is an online forum where local people discuss where they find the best prices on fish, wine, meat and eating out in their local areas.

Deals of the week

Each supermarket will feature its latest deals on its website, whether weekly or daily. It's worth taking a peek at your store's website before you go shopping; if you have time, look at the nearest rival's website too to see just what's on offer.

The Foreign Legion

The native food store stalwarts are facing stiff – and increasingly public – competition from the likes of German supermarkets Netto, Lidl and Aldi, whose self-proclaimed 'hypermarkets' are springing up all over the UK and starting to make inroads into North America. Aldi's most recent UK TV campaign declares that fresh vegetables are all available for 69p, while Lidl has smartened up its act and was recently crowned 'Best value for money retailer 2008' by UK consumers' association Which?. Are they really able to offer better prices for quality food?

What's Hot and What's Not

There's a great survey available online from journalist Martin Lewis. His research into what's hot and what's not at Aldi, Lidl and Netto aims to find the best products at the best prices – and helps you to avoid falling into the trap of thinking that just because something is cheap, it is worth buying. You can read it here: www.moneysavingexpert.com/shopping/are-cheap-supermarkets-good.

Unknown Quantity

These stores may seem to be out of your usual comfort zone, but in the hunt for the best prices, here are a few helpful hints to guide you through alien aisles:

Language

Don't be put off by the fact that labels are in German or Polish – most have translations into English.

Unfamiliarity

Also, don't be misled into thinking that just because it's not a US or UK brand with which we are familiar, then it can't be any good. Tinned fruit cocktails are going to be the same in Warsaw as in Wyoming. Oranges are oranges wherever you go in the world.

The stores don't always look as clearly laid out as mainstream supermarkets, with their glitzy cabinets and polished aisles, but that sort of pretty layout is often factored into the extra price you pay at more upmarket establishments.

Bring Your Own Bags

If you don't come with several plastic bags, you will have to pay for these at the counter.

Party Food at Low Prices

Frozen food stores and these cheaper Continental outlets are brilliant for bulk-buy snack foods and party mix.

Iceland

Iceland, for example, often will do a best price deal, giving customers three packets of finger food for £5 – which can feed 12 people with a selection of hot savouries.

Lidl

Lidl does a great range of Christmas fare: bags of soft, traditional pepper-cookies which last for ages and smell divine, massive bags of honey roast nuts and super deals on cakes. To buy the same 'imported' range of Germanic confectionery from the more mainstream supermarkets, you will pay significantly more for no better quality.

Customer Comment: A Happy Shopper

Lucy, 19, a student from London says: 'I now go to Lidl and Aldi for most of my shopping. Now they do know how to discount.'

Markets

There is a lot of value to be gained from leaving your fruit and vegetable purchases to the local Indian grocery shop or your cheese and meat purchases for the Saturday morning market. Markets are sometimes bypassed in this busy age of instant consumerism, but the thrill of meandering through rows of multicoloured fruit is something to be experienced just for the sake of it. The fact that there is always the potential for best price bargains at markets makes it all the more appealing.

Fruit and Veg

Because market stalls charge according to weight and/or quantity, rather than for packaging and presentation, you will save money by getting just the right portions you want, without wasting anything.

More For Your Money

Some exotic fruit, such as mangoes, are cheaper in markets or local grocery stores than in supermarkets. For example, £1 may get you two to three ripe mangoes from a local market stall; they retail in supermarkets and other stores from 69p to £1.20 each.

Paying for Packaging

Try this challenge – buy a packet of tomatoes from a supermarket and the same number of fresh ones, loose from a market stall. The market stall's local produce will usually work out to be the best price for (usually) fresher goods.

Take the Taste Test

For example, strawberries from a farmer's market are no more expensive than Asda or Tesco – but the taste is sensational, the smell is amazing and they're so toothsome you might want to buy more.

Organic Food

You will not pay supermarket prices for buying fresh, home-grown, organic produce from a local marketplace.

Upmarket Markets

Borough Market, London, is a specialist in fruit and vegetables, cheeses and fine ciders; it is open Thursdays, 11 a.m.–5 p.m., Fridays, 12 p.m.–6 p.m. and Saturdays, 9 a.m.–4 p.m. This

market is getting cult status among the more well-to-do Londoners, however, so not every stall will offer a bargain buy, so take a look around first before you make your purchases.

Meat and Fish

Two London markets – Billingsgate Fish Market, open Tuesday to Saturday 5 a.m.–8.30 a.m., and Smithfield Meat Market, open Monday to Friday, 4 a.m.–12 p.m. – are great places to get those special steaks or fresh salmon for bargain prices. You can be fooled into thinking that quality cuts at supermarkets are cheap because they are offering special deals, or pledging low prices. But where do they get their meat from? Cut out the middleman and go straight to the wholesalers. You could save pounds off your dinner party or Christmas fare.

Other Food Shops

Supermarkets and markets are some of the obvious places to get your regular food shop, and they are the places we visit most often. But there are of course a multitude of locations that sell food, some of which may have some advantages – you just have to work out if those advantages include saving you money.

Specialist Food Stores

Most supermarkets offer food from around the world to cater for increasingly diverse tastes. But there are also many independent delicatessens springing up which can sometimes give you more choice for your money.

Wider Range of Goods

Polish, Mediterranean and Caribbean shops have their own wholesales, in-depth knowledge of the produce and often a far better range of foodstuffs to suit your differing budgets.

'Bulk Barn' Outlets

These outlets for Chinese or Thai food are excellent for finding best prices on large, bulk products such as sauces or rice, which you would not get in supermarkets.

Purchasing Power

Supermarkets, however, often have the advantage of size so can buy even speciality foods at a better discount: a saving that is usually passed onto consumers.

Local Shops for Local People

These can sometimes offer good value for money on certain items such as bags of spices or loose, often more exotic, vegetables and dried fruit. But perhaps the best value you get from your corner store is customer recognition and the odd favour they will do for you, such as a free cake on your way home, or waiving the odd £1 or 50p. Don't try this if you don't show them any loyalty.

So Can You Save?

Probably not, so don't be tempted too often. Sometimes it's not worth going into them at all to look at their prices because of the shopkeeper's tendency to follow you round the aisles. The following might be your experience, too:

'I'm researching prices for an article on how consumers can find the lowest prices for their groceries. I wonder if you might, please, tell me how you keep your prices competitive?'
'Get out of my shop.'

Customer Comment: Give Them a Chance

Rebecca May, King's College medical student from London, UK, says: 'Sometimes my local corner shop costs less for fruit and vegetables than the bigger stores, although the bigger stores don't charge so much for bread, milk or butter – so it depends what you are looking for.'

General Stores

Sometimes, it is worth thinking outside the trolley when it comes to looking for the bargains. Where else, apart from markets and supermarkets, can you find best prices on certain goods? Here are a few for starters:

Bargain Shops

Poundland, the Dollar Store, Dollarama, Euroland... these international cheap-as-chips/fries/frites shops are becoming the busy mother's best friends.

Offers

General stores have great offers on packet foods at certain times. For example, Woolworth's 'well worth it' range has recently extended to Champagne, for £5 per bottle, a box of chocolates for £1 and traditional favourite sweets at rock-bottom prices.

A Few Examples

In such stores, you can find the following:

✔ **Confectionery:** Large packets of biscuits for £1, bags of packet mix or party sweets, large bars of Toblerone.

✔ **Packet foods:** Cup-a-Soups, tinned soups, jars of mustard, three-for-one deals on spices and packet sauces for £1.

✔ **Savoury snacks:** 1-kg packs of mixed nuts, tubs of Twiglets, multi-packs of crisps.

Three Warnings Apply

✔ **Don't be fooled:** Not everything is a best buy just because it's in a cheap store and has a £1 sticker. Sometimes, the foodstuff is cheaper in supermarkets. For example, an average-sized box of dried cat food retails between 70p to 90p rather than £1.

✔ **Low quality:** Some of the no-brand, cheap chocolates, wine and champagne are not worth buying. A supermarket's own brand may be dearer, but will not taste like sugary pulp (this applies to chocolates) or slightly gassy vinegar (vis-à-vis cheap booze).

✔ **Out of date:** Many of the food products will retail for £1 in these stores because they are at, or even past, the sell-by date. Make sure you check the labels so that you are not buying goods way past their use-by dates.

Happy Shoppers

You may be thinking: 'Are all supermarkets out to get me?', or 'Will I be taken for a ride by a market stall owner?' Not at all. But supermarkets are not there to be your best friend, they are there to sell products. And while many of them rightly claim to be able to offer you the best price, whether because of their bulk purchasing power or a special short-term deal, it's worth establishing a process that you can apply whenever you go shopping.

Top Tips

Here are a few helpful tips to guide you towards the best prices and the real deals:

The Pre-Shopping List

Keep a note of the prices you pay for your regular items at different stores. You may find it worth your while to make smaller trips to different shops if you live locally, or it may be expedient to drive to a different supermarket in order to save several pounds.

Timing Is Everything

Be prepared to change your shopping patterns. Most supermarkets start discounts (sometimes set by head office, sometimes by the store itself) from 10 a.m. in the morning, but the real discounts will appear after 7 p.m. The early birds do not always get the worm.

Store Cards

If points mean prizes, and all you have to do is remember to bring the card to scan in when you go shopping, then do so. Redeem the points at peak times – parties, Easter, Christmas and other celebrations – to maximize your discount at a time when it really matters to you.

Bake Your Own

Why would you buy easy-to-make snacks such as Kellogg's Rice Krispie Chewy Squares at nearly £1.60 for a packet of four? Sure, they're tasty, but why not buy a no-frills box of the right sort of cereal and a £1 (or cheaper) bag of marshmallows and make your own – with plenty of cereal left over for several breakfasts. Best price AND something fun to do.

Bypass the Bargain Bin

Ignore next-to-the-tills eye candy. It's not only the children who are attracted by the sweeties at their eye level; many an adult has come undone at the sight of a 'bargain bin' near the queue. Is it really a bargain? Just because there's a big sign flashing up the price of those cheese straws does not mean they are cheap at that price.

Be Canny About Store Layouts

Fruit and nuts in the baking counter are often cheaper than the 'ready-to-eat' packets of nuts near the snack counters. For example, a 0.5 kg bag of cooking prunes can be 30 per cent less than a smaller, 'ready-to-eat' bag arranged temptingly by the sandwiches counter. The same goes for cooking almonds and mixed nuts.

The Shrinking Shop

These are difficult times for supermarkets, especially as they have to placate twitchy shareholders as well as keeping their custom. So some manufacturers and shops may 'shrink ray' their goods but still charge the same price. In August, leading brand Cadbury's admitted to shrinking the size of its multi-pack chocolate bars from 250 g to 230 g, but were still charging the original £1.38 average price. Strongbow, the cider brewer, kept the same price on its new 15-pack of cans as it had charged for the bigger, 18-pack.

Stick to a Budget

Try calculating the amount of money you will need for the shopping list you have prepared, then take that amount out in cash. Unless you can get Airmiles or points on your credit card, use cash – you will be far less tempted to go off-piste with any tempting eye-level goodies.

Shop When You're Satisfied

Don't food shop when you're hungry. You'll dive into the nearest store, buy more than you need and pay less heed to both price and the nutritional value of your food.

Buy Loose, Local Produce

Do try to support your markets and local stores by getting fresh vegetables and fruit there – it is often much cheaper and probably locally grown too, rather than being flown in from South Africa. Your mushrooms should not travel further to get to the store than you do. Organic food can cost more in supermarkets, but if you go to a local farmer's market, it won't be so costly to eat a little more healthily while supporting your local farmers.

The Shopping Club

Local shopping groups are being formed by small groups of friends who shop together to make the most of special offers and discounts. By apportioning BOGOF and similar deals between them, pooling coupons and sharing one car to get to the supermarket, their shopping bills are getting smaller and they are able to make the most out of special deals and short-term, best-buy prices.

Buy Bigger

Often, bigger is better – that is, it will give you a better price per unit of produce. For example, you may get more for your money by buying a large bottle of squash than by getting the usual smaller size, or pay less per vitamin for a large pack than for a smaller one.

Case Study: No Crying Over Milk Spilled

One family in Coulsdon buys six to eight one-pint bottles of milk rather than three big ones. The reason behind this is that, with four children, the milk will get spilled, or sometimes go to waste. But assuming the average market price of one pint of milk is 42p (average across Tesco, Asda, Sainsbury's and Marks & Spencer, as at 20 August 2008); 6 x 42p = £2.52.

The average price of a two-pint bottle of milk across these four stores is 80p (the milk price war of 50p notwithstanding). Three bottles of this size milk works out at £2.40 – a saving of 12p.

The best suggestion made to this family was to keep a couple of clean, empty one-pint bottles and pour the milk from a two-pint bottle into these, saving the mother the hassle of clearing up any spills, and generating a saving of 12p per week. And 12p x 52 weeks in a year = £6.24 worth of savings.

Check the Labels

Bigger may mean a better price than buying individual items, but make sure you're getting the same goods for your money as previously; otherwise the 'best price' savings on such items may be deceptive. Always read the labels to see what you are actually getting.

Reaping What You Sow

In these hard times for consumers, it's easy to get misled by brightly-coloured signs touting what you think are best price buys. It's also tempting to rush for the nearest shop for convenience, even though you know that you could get your shopping more cheaply elsewhere.

But by doing a bit of research, sticking to a budget, using your club cards and being clever about how and when and where you shop, you will find it a lot easier on your pocket. All this may seem like hard work, but when you consider the savings you will make for doing a little bit more homework and taking advantage of the right offers, it really will pay off. To paraphrase one supermarket – every little really does help.

Household

Cleaning Products

Open the cupboard under the kitchen sink and chances are that it is packed with cleaning and laundry products, most of which you only use occasionally. The purchases can bump up your grocery bill considerably, so think about what you really need, what you can do without and where you can make savings. One way of saving money is to make your own cleaners using things like white vinegar – see the book *100 Ways to Beat the Credit Crunch*, in the same series, for advice on this.

The Essential Cleaning Kit

You need surprisingly few items in your cleaning cupboard, as some have a multitude of uses. Must-haves include washing-up liquid, bleach, cream cleaner, spray cleaner, washing and dishwasher powder, liquid or capsules, fabric conditioner and cloths.

Opt for Own-Label Items

Own-brand items are usually significantly cheaper, and some have even beaten pricier brand names in consumer tests. With brands, you generally pay more for the name, reputation and choice of fragrances.

Get Branded Products for Less

If you prefer to use tried and trusted brands, log on to supermarket comparison website www.mysupermarket.com to find out where you can get the best possible prices.

Buy Larger Sizes

Buy bigger packs which are nearly always better value, and look out for 'buy one, get one free' and other offers.

Buy Economy Lines

Some of the major supermarkets, including Tesco and Morrisons, stock no-frills economy ranges of household and other products. These are labelled as 'value' products and are even cheaper than similar, own-label items.

Shop in Discount Supermarkets

You may not recognize the product names, but prices are consistently low in Lidl, Netto and Aldi, so try out their cleaning products to see how they match up to your usual brand.

Reusable Cleaning Aids

A drive towards combining money-saving and environmentally-friendly features has led to the production of reusable products which reduce the need for chemical cleaners. Although the initial outlay is higher, they are very long-lasting, so you will make great savings long-term.

Microfibre Cloths

Made from millions of tiny fibres, these cloths just require water to clean all hard surfaces and are especially good for stainless steel. They cost around £5 each, are machine washable and last for years.

Wash Balls

Pop these in your washing machine and they provide extra scrubbing action, so you can reduce the amount of soap powder by 75 per cent. Try Dolly Wash Balls, from www.lakeland.co.uk, or Aqua Balls from www.thegreenstoreonline.co.uk, among many others.

Dryer Balls

These are used in the tumble dryer, but cut out the need for adding fabric conditioner to the wash. They gently massage fibres while they dry, leaving clothes, towels and bed linen beautifully soft; from Lakeland or Amazon among many others.

Furniture

Furniture is a major investment and needs to be chosen carefully to ensure that it is good value, suits your home and your needs, and stays looking good for a long time to come. Whether you are after pieces for your living room, dining room or bedroom, the good news is that there are plenty of places where you can find them for less.

Sofas and Armchairs

Sofas and armchairs vary tremendously in price. Know what to look out for when making your purchase to make your money go further.

Know Your Construction

Whether you are aiming for a reduction on a quality product that is built to last, or a cheap, budget version, find out how it is constructed, so you know that you are getting value for money.

✓ **Top-end sofas**: These consist of a hardwood frame with screwed, glued or dowelled joints. They have coil-sprung seats and feather and down or feather and fibre cushions.

✓ **Mid-priced sofas**: These have hardwood frames with zigzag springs, and foam or feather and fibre cushions.

✓ **Budget sofas**: These have softwood frames with webbing and foam padding, and cushions are filled with foam.

What Size?

It goes without saying that a bigger sofa costs more, so think about how many people will be sitting on it on a regular basis. If the answer is one or two, ask yourself whether it is worth paying more for extra seating you will rarely use.

Sofa Beds

Sofa beds are dearer than standard sofas, and are worthwhile investments if there is no other spare bed. However, if a sofa bed is unlikely to be used, there is no point paying extra for it.

Replacement Covers

If your sofa or armchair is tatty rather than worn out, a new cover will give it a fresh lease of life and costs far less than replacing it completely.

✔ **Contact the manufacturer or store**: Find out whether replacement covers are available.

✔ **Bemz**: Bemz stocks a well-priced range of covers for IKEA upholstery – visit www.Bemz.com.

✔ **Make**: Buy some upholstery fabric and get a seamstress to make the cover for you.

Beds

A bed needs to be supportive and comfortable, so try it out with your partner where possible. If the frame or divan base is in good condition, save money by replacing the mattress only and go for the best that you can afford (and never buy second-hand). You have the choice of sprung, memory foam and latex mattresses, though you will usually pay less for a top-quality pocket sprung version than for basic latex or memory foam.

Storage

When kitting out an entire bedroom, go for a divan bed with storage drawers underneath, which will work out cheaper than buying a separate chest of drawers.

Cabinet Furniture

This encompasses all types of solid wood or MDF furniture, including dining room tables and chairs, coffee tables, bookcases, wardrobes and chests of drawers.

Flat-Pack

You have the option of flat-pack or ready assembled furniture when buying new. Flat-pack is cheaper as you are not paying to have it assembled.

Buy in Sets

Purchasing sets – such as a table and four chairs – works out cheaper than buying individual items separately.

Modular Pieces

Built-in, fitted furniture is great for small homes as it maximizes every inch of space, but works out far more expensive than buying separate, freestanding pieces. Modular units, which can be mixed and matched to create a bespoke storage system, are a far cheaper compromise.

General Tips

Spread Payments

When buying new, ask about the availability of interest-free credit which will enable you to spread payments over a period of time.

Buy in Good Condition

Check second-hand, wooden furniture carefully for signs of woodworm as you will have very little recourse once you have paid.

Haggle

It is always worth haggling for a discount in price, or to get something else thrown in free – for example, cushions or a headboard

Think About Delivery

It's easy to forget to add the cost of delivery on to your purchase, so check out the delivery situation before you buy.

- **Second-hand:** Buyers are nearly always liable for delivery charges when buying second-hand items – and you might have to arrange transport.

- **Negotiate:** Some companies charge as much as £50 for delivering large items of furniture, so see if this fee can be negotiated. If delivery is included in the price, ask for a reduction if you offer to collect it yourself.

- **Returns:** Find out whether furniture can be returned free of charge if you buy it unseen from an online or mail order company.

Where to Buy Furniture

Ex-Show Home

Find new furniture which has previously been on display in show homes at a fraction of its original price in a specialist showroom. These sell thousands of items and stock changes frequently, so you will need to visit in person. Measure before buying, as some items such as sofas and beds are smaller than standard to make the rooms they have been displayed in look bigger. Try:

- **The Showhome Warehouse:** www.showhomewarehouse.co.uk, Northamptonshire.

- **ExShowhouse Furniture:** www.exshowhousefurniture.com, Glasgow.

- **Trading Interiors:** 020 8397 4730, Glasgow.

Shop In-Store

A huge advantage of shopping in-store is that you can see and try what you are buying, and even take it away with you.

✅ **IKEA:** Since it opened in the UK in 1987, IKEA has revolutionized the way we buy furniture. It offers bargain, contemporary designs that you can take away or have delivered. All cabinet furniture is flat-pack.

✅ **John Lewis:** This store has a reputation for quality and sells own- and leading brands at competitive prices.

✅ **DFS:** This upholstery specialist regularly holds half-price sales.

✅ **Trade Secret:** This company sells cancelled orders and returned furniture at half the high street price from four showrooms in the Home Counties; see www.trade-secret.co.uk.

✅ **National Brands:** This family run business, www.national-brands.co.uk, runs two massive discount furniture warehouses in Liverpool and Cambridge.

Buy Online

Dozens of websites sell low-priced furniture, so put some time aside to surf the net and get an idea of the vast range on offer. Amongst the best are:

✅ **www.direct.tesco.com:** Offers free delivery on orders over £50 and buy one, get one free deals on selected ranges.

✅ **www.argos.co.uk:** Has a vast range of low-priced furniture. Large items can be delivered cheaply.

- ✅ **www.Furniture123.co.uk**: An easy to navigate site with a vast stock and regular clearance sales.

- ✅ **www.dwell.co.uk**: Features sleek, contemporary designs at affordable prices.

- ✅ **www.furniturebusters.com**: Sells brand names for less.

Opt For Ex-Display Items

Furniture that is out on display may be reduced to half price or less, so ask if it is for sale. Check it carefully and ask for a further reduction if you find any damage – and are happy to buy something that is shop-soiled.

Head for a Factory Shop

Buying at a factory shop enables you to access some otherwise unaffordable brands, and you have the added bonus of knowing you are getting a top-quality product that is built to last. The savings you can make on bigger purchases can more than justify the travel costs, though ask about delivery well in advance of your trip. Visit:

- ✅ **Habitat**: Their clearance shop in Wythenshawe, Manchester, which specializes in furniture rather than accessories.

- ✅ **Wesley Barrell**: Their showroom in Witney, Oxfordshire, which has up to 50 per cent off selected handmade sofas and armchairs.

Attend an Auction

Buying at auction is an excellent way to find mainly second-hand, one-off pieces at knock-down prices. Read the catalogue, inspect pieces that catch your eye and register your interest with the auction house. Some tips are:

- ✅ **Know the system**: Sit in on a prior auction so you know how the system works.

☑ **Be strong**: Set yourself a limit and do not exceed it.

☑ **Be sure**: Once your bid is accepted, you have entered into a legally binding contract and you cannot change your mind.

☑ **Remember VAT**: When setting your budget, remember that you have to pay a premium of around 15 per cent, plus VAT, on the purchase price.

Bid Online

An online auction gives you access to millions of products. Always read product descriptions and feedback on sellers to minimize the risk of being ripped off.

Rummage Around Junk Shops

Junk shops are a good source of inexpensive second-hand furniture, particularly if you are willing to put in a little work – perhaps painting, stripping or changing handles. Shops in wealthier areas tend to have a better mix of products and it is always worth asking for a reduction.

Newspaper and Online Advertisements

Local papers and classified sites such as www.gumtree.com are packed with advertisements for second-hand, and occasionally new, furniture. Arrange to meet the seller face to face and never hand over money before you have seen the item, as you will not have the security of a buyer protection scheme.

Get it for Free

The recycling culture means that some people prefer to give away old furniture rather than consign it to a tip. You are unlikely to find designer cast-offs this way, but you may get lucky and find something in reasonable condition, ideal for a first, student or rental flat, that is absolutely free. For further information, visit www.uk.freecycle.org.

Fabrics, Textiles and Soft Furnishings

You can give your home a whole new look with carefully chosen curtains, cushions, throws and other soft furnishing, which are easy to find at heavily discounted prices. And if you are a dab hand at sewing, make even greater savings by buying bargain fabrics off the roll and running up the items yourself.

Buying Tips

Do your homework and take time to examine fabrics carefully to ensure you get value for money.

Seconds

Fabrics marked as seconds are reduced for a reason, but this might be because they are last season's stock or have tiny imperfections which can barely be seen. Check for loose or pulled threads, uneven edges and other flaws, and make sure colour is consistent throughout.

Colour Match Separate Items

When buying separate items such as towels or cushions, check that colours are a good match.

Buy Dressmaking Fabric

Use dressmaking rather than curtain fabric to make lightweight curtains – it is often far cheaper and there may be a greater choice.

Opt for Double Width

If there is a choice, buy double rather than standard with fabric, which goes twice as far and only costs a little more.

Buy More Than You Need

If you fall for a particular fabric, buy more than you need as you are unlikely to find it again.

Make Cushion Covers from Remnants

Fabric remnants can sometimes be picked up for next to nothing, and you will need less than a metre to make a cushion cover.

Buy Cushion Covers Only

There is no need to waste money buying new cushion pads – buy covers only and slip the old pads inside.

Buy a Bundle

Towels are often sold in bundles of three or four, which work out far cheaper than buying individually.

Where to Buy

You can find bargain textiles in a whole host of locations, from supermarkets to shopping villages.

Supermarkets

Virtually all the major supermarkets feature seasonal collections of low-priced soft furnishings, including cushions, towels and bed linen. Check out George at Asda, Tu at Sainsbury's and own-label collections at Tesco and Morrisons.

Discount Specialist Shops

These permanent outlets, which sell online, via showrooms or both, can afford to keep prices low as they are selling direct to the public. Some of the lines are produced by leading manufacturers, at a fraction of the price of named brands. Check out:

 www.fabricworldlondon.co.uk

 www.homelinen.co.uk

 www.knickerbean.com

www.kingofcotton.co.uk

 www.curtainfactoryoutlet.co.uk

Factory Shops

Many leading brands sell discontinued lines, surplus stock and last season's ranges at huge discounts in one-off factory shops and shopping villages.

 Laura Ashley: The factory shop in Hornsea, East Yorkshire, stocks bed linen and fabrics.

 Cath Kidston: Find the outlet at Bicester Shopping Village.

 Sanderson: The factory shop in Central Manchester stocks seconds in furnishing fabrics, plus curtains and bed linen at half price.

Discount Stores

Primark, Matalan and Dunelm Mill stock inexpensive ranges of own-brand towels, bed linen and cushions. Towels are sold at several price points – buy one notch up from the very cheapest for excellent value without compromising on quality.

Buy Quality Drapes Second-Hand

Save money on window dressings by shopping at a branch of The Curtain Exchange, where you will find high quality, lined curtains, often in designer fabrics. The reason why prices are far lower than you would expect is because these curtains are second-hand, though all are in excellent condition. Log on to www.thecurtainexchange.net for more information.

Tableware, China and Glass

While tableware and glasses are essential elements in every home, individual pieces such as vases and jugs can be used to add personality and interest. Whether you are shopping for fine china or everyday items, there are plenty of places where you can find them for less.

Buying Tips

Unless boxed up, always examine glass, ceramics and china for chips and cracks.

Seconds

Items are marked as such because they might have imperfections such as uneven glaze, barely visible bubbles, spots or colour that is slightly out of kilter. Seconds are usually sold as seen, so you will be unable to return them later if you discover a flaw.

Boxed Sets

Boxed sets cost less than buying individual pieces. Ensure you are not paying for pieces you do not need, such as separate soup and cereal bowls if you only use one type of bowl.

Discontinued Ranges

Crockery sets are often substantially reduced when they are about to be discontinued, so ask if this is the case and check whether replacements will be available in case of breakages. If not, you will be able to get them via a china matching service, but this can be pricey.

Where to Buy

High Street Stores

Find anything from reduced lines of premium bone china in department stores, through to great value starter packs of tableware in IKEA, Woolworths, Asda and Tesco.

Factory Shops

China, ceramic and glassware brands are particularly well represented in the factory shop sector – possibly because the manufacturing process always produces a certain quota of products with minor imperfections, which can be sold as seconds, with huge reductions. Among the best are:

- **Wedgwood factory shop**: This also stocks crystal brands, at discounts of up to 75 per cent. Visit www.wedgwoodfactoryshop.com.

- **Spode factory shop**: Fine bone china at reduced prices. Visit www.spode.co.uk.

- **Emma Bridgewater factory outlet**: This stocks a wide range of seconds and discontinued lines, plus tableware and textiles. Visit www.emmabridgewater.co.uk.

- **Villeroy and Boch**: This company has factory outlets in several shopping villages and a stand-alone shop, with discounts of up to 80 per cent. Visit www.villeroy-boch.com.

- **Dartington Crystal**: Dartington has around a dozen factory shops, selling seconds and perfect crystal glassware at huge discounts. Visit www.dartington.co.uk.

Car Boot Sales

What you find at car boot sales is completely a matter of luck, but they are great hunting grounds for quirky, one-off pieces and complete and incomplete sets of old china. You will have the pick of the bargains if you arrive early, but vendors are more likely to reduce prices further towards the end of the sale, when they want to sell everything and get away. You will find details of car boot sales in local papers, or look online at www.carbootjunction.com.

Holiday Buys

In Mediterranean countries, markets and even souvenir stalls are great places to pick up inexpensive, colourful bowls, dishes and jugs that look wonderful on the table alongside plain white china. Make sure these are carefully wrapped before you travel home and keep them in your hand baggage if possible, as they will not be such a bargain if they arrive home in smithereens.

Flooring

Make sure you select the right type of flooring for the room in question, then consider where you can find it cheaper. Options include carpets and natural floor coverings, such as coir and sisal, or you may prefer wood, stone or other hard flooring.

Carpet

Suitable for all areas apart from kitchens and bathrooms, which are prone to getting wet, carpet is available in a wide range of textures, weaves and prices.

Save with Synthetic

All-wool carpets are the most luxurious, but hard-wearing synthetic ones cost far less, though do not keep their looks for as long. A 50:50 wool/synthetic mix is a practical compromise.

Natural Flooring

Coir is the most reasonably priced natural flooring and, like carpet, is unsuitable for wet areas and needs to be fitted by a professional. It feels slightly rough – something to bear in mind if you like to walk around barefoot.

Fitting

You will need to pay a professional to fit the carpet, but many retailers offer fitting as part of the service, which costs less than buying the carpet and sourcing an independent fitter.

Underlay

Buy new underlay or the carpet will wear unevenly, but you may be able to find it more cheaply in a DIY shed than at the carpet retailer.

Wooden Flooring

Wooden flooring looks good, wears well and is suitable for most rooms. Again, prices vary according to the type you go for.

Real Wood?

Solid wood can be pricey, but engineered wood and wood-effect laminates look just like the real thing and are far cheaper.

Do-It-Yourself

As long as the subfloor underneath is fairly even, you will be able to fit a wood or laminate floor yourself, as long as you are reasonably competent at DIY.

Stone Floors

Limestone and terracotta are durable, but expensive, and generally most suitable for downstairs rooms. Some types of real stone need treating to protect them from stains, which bumps up the cost.

Making Savings

If your heart is set on stone, opt for slate tiles which are less expensive than other types. Choose cheaper quarry tiles instead of terracotta, or go for a convincing ceramic or laminate lookalike.

Vinyl

Vinyl flooring, in sheets or tiles, is the least expensive of all and is available in a wide range of designs, patterns and finishes, including ones which bear a striking resemblance to wood and stone.

Where to Buy

Look out for reductions on end-of-lines and carpet remnants in independent stores. Try also:

- **DIY sheds:** Stores including Wickes, B&Q and Homebase are a good source of inexpensive wood, laminates and tiles.

- **Topps Tiles:** Topps has a vast stock of tiles, stone, wooden and laminate flooring at value for money prices. Visit www.toppstiles.co.uk.

- **Carpetright:** This store stocks low-cost laminate and vinyl flooring as well as carpets, in its 450 stores, plus extra discounts online. Visit www.carpetright.co.uk.

- **Rugzone:** Priding itself on low prices across hundreds of products, Rugzone offers to double the difference in price if you find the same rug cheaper. Visit www.rugzone.co.uk.

- **Cheap underlay:** Find carpet underlay at trade prices at www.discounted-carpet-underlay.co.uk.

Kitchens and Bathrooms

Kitchen and bathroom upgrades are some of the most popular home improvements, but you do not need to spend a fortune to make a vast difference. Huge discounts are available if you are opting for a complete refit, or you may prefer a simple revamp instead.

New Kitchens

There are plenty of places to find a brand new kitchen for less, including sales, factory shops and ex-display units.

Discounts

Savings of 50 per cent or more are not uncommon in this competitive market, so always shop in sale time.

- **Magnet, Moben and MFI**: These offer particularly good discounts.

- **IKEA**: Low-priced kitchens in a variety of contemporary designs can be had at IKEA.

- **Kitchens Direct**: Good value kitchens are sold and fitted by Kitchens Direct. Visit www.kitchensdirect.co.uk.

- **Try the DIY superstores**: B&Q, Wickes and Homebase offer great deals on their own-brand kitchens.

- **Ex-display**: They may be shop-soiled, but ex-display units can be found for less than half price.

Free Plan

Get your kitchen planned for free before you make up your mind. Take along a scale drawing, including measurements, to the showroom, and you will be given a 3D plan of what your new kitchen will look like.

Negotiate

Be prepared to haggle – ask whether the retailer will include additional units, worktops or appliances in the price.

Fitting

Fitting costs are not usually included in the price of the kitchen, so have a go yourself or employ your own contractors. Inexpensive units tend to be flat-packed, so you will need to assemble them yourself or get your fitter to do so.

Kitchen Updates

Revamping your existing kitchen costs far less than replacing it, so think about what you can do to give it a new look on a budget.

Swap the Doors

If the carcass is in good condition, replacing the doors only will make a real difference. Try a specialist replacement door company that offers low prices, such as www.kitchenrefurbs.co.uk.

Replace Worktops

Laminates are the cheapest option when replacing kitchen worktops and can look just as good as far more expensive composites. Find low prices at Wickes and www.kitchen-worktops-plus.co.uk.

Bathrooms

Bathroom suites have tumbled in price and you can find a new one for under £200 in DIY superstores or specialist outlets.

Plumber's Merchants Discounts

Try plumbers' merchants for great deals – they sell to the public as well, but remember that VAT is added on afterwards.

Discounts Online

You will find numerous bathroom discount companies online. The Bathroom Discount Centre, www.bathdisc.co.uk and Bathstore, www.bathstore.com have keen prices and their own showrooms, so you can see what you are buying before you commit.

Buying Tips

- **Built-in**: Built-in baths cost less than freestanding ones.

- **Separate installation**: Some companies offer installation as part of the package, but you may pay less if you find your own plumber.

- **Just the taps**: If your suite is in good condition, replace dated bathroom and basin taps with contemporary ones for a classier look. Colourwash, www.colourwash.co.uk sells designer-style taps and other accessories at high street prices.

Decorating and DIY materials

From paints and wallpaper to timber and bricks, there are many ways to make savings when shopping for DIY materials. Work out exactly what you need, then compare prices online and in local stores to find out where the best bargains are.

Tips and Tricks

Mix Your Own Colours

Adding a match pot of colour to cheap white emulsion costs less than buying a larger tin, but test the shade out first and mix as much as you need as it will be hard to make a colour match later.

Use Match Pots on Feature Walls

Match pots cost a fraction of the price of larger paint cans, so buy these if you are only painting a small area.

Buy Reclaimed Materials

Reclaimed bricks and timber cost less than new.

Where to Buy

 Surplus: Buy surplus recycled building materials for less at www.whatdoidowiththis.com. Find and swap surplus materials at www.tradeleftovers.com.

Salvage: Visit architectural salvage yards for period fittings at low cost.

Skips: Check out skips for doors, timber and bricks which have been dumped.

Trade: Pay trade prices by buying from builders' and timber yards, and negotiate a discount by buying in bulk.

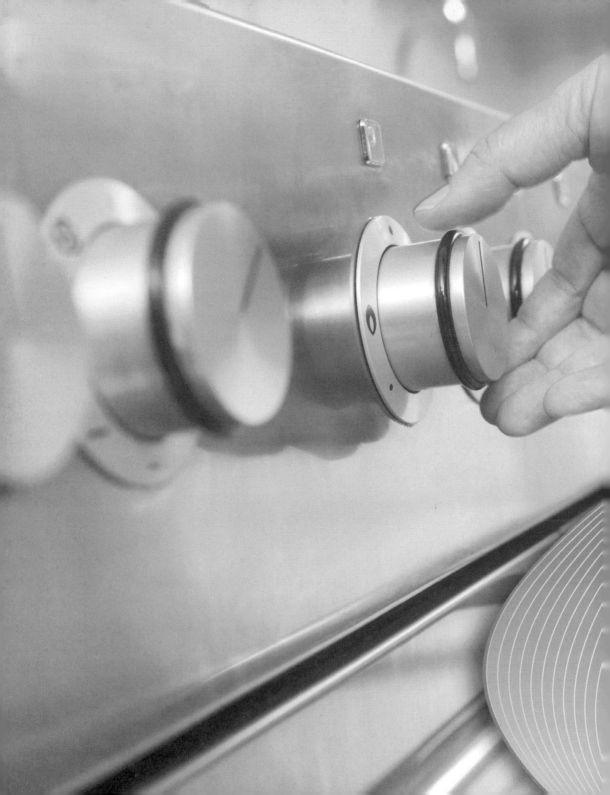

Appliances
& Electronics

White Goods

Hefty markups and keen competition for kitchen appliances – commonly referred to as white goods – mean that substantial discounts are widely available. All but the most basic appliances incorporate a whole host of features so, before you start shopping, decide what your requirements are, as there is no point in paying more for ones you never use.

Keep Costs Down

Whichever type of appliance you are buying, there are a number of ways you can reduce your outlay.

Big v. Basic Brands

There are so many brands in this sector that prices vary a lot. If you buy a top-end name, such as Bosch, AEG or Miele, you are paying extra for better reliability and more advanced technology, which mean long-term savings on running costs and repair bills.

Consider Energy Efficiency

Appliances are graded from A to G for energy efficiency and performance, with A being the most economical. Pricier appliances are generally more efficient, so running costs will be lower.

Stick to White

White products usually cost less than equivalent models in stainless steel, chrome or coloured finishes.

Go for Freestanding Appliances

These are cheaper than built-in or integrated models, and you can take them with you when you move house.

Choose a Two-in-One

Combined fridge-freezers and washer-dryers cost less than buying two separate models.

Opt for Standard Sizes

Most appliances are a standard 60 cm (23$\frac{1}{2}$ in) wide, though many manufacturers also make compact sizes, designed for smaller kitchens. Despite their limited proportions, they cost the same or even more, so a standard sized model will provide better value for money.

Check Delivery and Installation Charges

Find out how much the supplier will charge for delivery and whether installation is included in the price. You will need to dispose of your old appliance, so again factor in collection costs – or save money by taking it to the local recycling centre yourself.

Buy More Than One

You will be in a much better position to ask for an additional discount if buying more than one appliance.

Fridges and Freezers

Cooling appliances range from basic larder designs through to American-style fridge freezers with chillers, salad crispers and iced water dispensers.

Choose a Chest Freezer

If a combined fridge-freezer does not provide all the freezer space you need, a separate chest freezer is more economical than an upright version. It takes up more space, though, so store it in the garage or utility room.

Opt for a Freezer on Top

Combined fridge-freezers are usually cheaper when the freezer is on top – though this does mean you will need to bend down to reach the fridge.

Home Laundry

Opt for a combined washer-dryer unless you frequently need to wash and dry at the same time. Dryers are expensive to run and tend to be slightly slower in combined machines – something to bear in mind if you prefer to tumble-dry all your laundry.

Top Loaders

These cost less than front-loading machines, but do not suit every home as they require free space above, so cannot slot in under a worktop.

Cookers and Hobs

Again, a combined, freestanding, all-in-one cooker costs less to buy than separate, built-in ovens and hobs.

Fuel Options

Most cookers are electric, gas or dual fuel – a gas hob with an electric oven. All-electric are cheaper to buy but more expensive to run. Halogen and induction hobs are sleek and easy to clean – but you pay a premium for this convenience.

Range Cookers

Range cookers are fashionable, but pricey. Most feature at least five hobs and a double or large oven, so unless you have a large family or entertain frequently, do not be tempted to place looks over economy.

Dishwashers

Not a necessity, but anyone who has one will wonder how they ever managed without it.

Capacity

Manufacturers claim that dishwashers use less energy than washing an equivalent number of dishes by hand. Buy one with a large capacity – 13 or 14 place settings – to reduce the running costs.

Programmes

In practice, most people only use two or three programmes, so look out for a model with fewer features that costs less.

Where to Buy White Goods

Whether you are shopping on the high street or online, there are dozens of outlets where you will find great deals.

Department Stores

Shop during sales for the best bargains. In some stores, it may be worth opening an account to take advantage of further discounts for new customers, but be sure to pay off the entire balance. John Lewis, in particular, is known for its keen pricing and stocks good value own brand white goods, as well as those from leading manufacturers.

Electrical Superstores

Most of these have both a high street and online presence. Look out for extra discounts and special clearances for online customers only.

 Comet: With its main website at www.comet.co.uk, Comet features special internet deals and even has its own clearance website at www.comet-clearance.co.uk, where you can bid for new, returned, ex-display, shop-soiled and refurbished products.

Currys: Currys has a vast range of appliances. Look out for the deal of the day for even greater savings. Visit www.currys.co.uk.

Online Superstores

These can afford to keep prices low as they do not have the overheads of running a showroom. Among the best are:

- www.amazon.co.uk
- www.empiredirect.co.uk
- www.appliancesonline.co.uk
- www.discount-appliances.co.uk
- www.dixons.co.uk

Supermarkets

Tesco and Sainsbury's both sell extensive ranges of white goods at competitive prices and you have the bonus of earning loyalty points on your purchase.

Independent Stores

Buyers and Sellers, www.buyersandsellersonline.co.uk, is one of the few retailers that manages to combine the personal service of an independent store with the range and competitive pricing you will find in a superstore. It also offers free delivery to all mainland addresses in the UK. Smaller outlets may not be able to compete with larger retailers in terms of price on every product, but it is worth asking if the manager is willing to do a deal, or throw in extra products when buying a specific item.

Kitchen Showrooms

If you are kitting out your entire kitchen, you may get a discount from the retailer if you buy your appliances there as well as the units. Be sure to price everything up so you know exactly how much you will be saving and whether you are better off sourcing them separately from a discount store.

Refurbished Appliances

Refurbished and reconditioned appliances are significantly cheaper than their brand new counterparts. However, you should only buy electricals from a reputable shop or website, such as Comet's clearance store. Although you may be tempted by prices on eBay or ads in your local paper, the items on offer could be dangerous, so this is a risk that is not worth taking.

Small Electricals

Vital to the smooth running of a household, these include essential products such as kettles, toasters and irons, and those that we find make life just that little bit easier. Microwaves, coffee makers, food processors and toasted sandwich makers all fall into the latter category.

Buying Tips

A recent survey from Halifax Home Insurance found that a quarter of a million British households have more than £500 worth of abandoned kitchen gadgets stored away, with toasted-sandwich makers topping the list. So before you part with your pounds, ask yourself whether you really need – or will use – the item you are planning to buy.

Settle for White

White plastic kettles and toasters are cheaper than metal ones and easier to wipe clean, too.

Buy a Set

Matching kettles and toasters are sometimes sold in sets, which cost less than buying each item individually.

Microwaves

You will pay a lot more for a microwave that is packed full of features, so go for a basic, cheaper model if you only ever use it for defrosting and reheating food.

Kettles With Water Filters

Kettles incorporating water filters cost more than those without, and on top of that you will have to lay out for cartridges which need to be changed about once a month. It is far cheaper to buy a more basic kettle and descale it on a regular basis.

Toasters

If you require a toaster simply to brown your bread, it is a waste of money to pay for advanced features that you never use, such as warming racks or extra-wide slots.

Irons

These range from bog-standard steam irons right through to steam generators that have detachable water tanks and can be used to freshen up curtains and upholstery in situ as well as press clothes. These

can cut ironing time in half as the high pressure steam irons both sides at once, but are only worth investing in if you spend a lot of time at the ironing board.

Filter Coffee Machines

Some machines filter coffee through a permanent or paper filter, while others use a pod system, where steam is forced through coffee in a disposable pod at high pressure. Pods may be easy to use, in that there are no messy grounds to throw away, but they also work out far more expensive than filters.

Vacuum Cleaners

It is entirely a matter of personal preference whether you go for an upright or cylinder model. Both types are available in bagless or traditional bagged versions, which tend to be slightly cheaper.

Where to Shop

As when buying larger appliances, there are plenty of places where you will find discounts, particularly on end-of-lines or old stock.

High Street

As well as department stores, take a look at low-priced, good-value ranges in Woolworths and Marks & Spencer, ideal for those setting up their first home. John Lewis's own brand is always worth a browse for its great designs at competitive prices.

Online Outlets and Superstores

Check out the following for cheap small electrical appliances:

 www.amazon.co.uk  **www.currys.co.uk**  **www.argos.co.uk**

Factory Shops

Find discontinued lines and seconds at:

 Salton Factory shops: Based in Manchester and Wolverhampton (call 0161 947 3000), these shops stock a variety of brands, including Russell Hobbs, Salton, Pifco and George Foreman. Products on offer include kettles, irons, steamers, clocks, deep fat fryers and toasters, all at rock bottom prices.

 The Werl Factory Shop: Based in Wolverhampton and at www.werl.co.uk, this shop has branded products from Rowenta, Tefal, Moulinex and Krups. The product range includes steam irons, steam generators, kettles, toasters, fryers, food processors, coffee makers, blenders, steam cookers and vacuum cleaners.

Second-Hand

You can pick up used electrical items in second-hand stores and at car boot sales for a fraction of the price you would pay for brand new, but there are important safety considerations to bear in mind:

Proof: When buying in a store, ask for proof from the seller that the item meets legal safety requirements.

Certification: Look for the approved marks – the CE mark, the BEAB mark, the BS safety mark or British Standard number when you buy electrical equipment.

Car boots: Never use an electrical item bought at a car boot sale without getting an electrician to check it out first. If you are going to have to pay someone to do this, the item is almost certainly not worth buying.

If in doubt: Do not buy anything if you have any doubts as to its safety.

Post-purchase: If you have already bought an appliance and it appears to be faulty, stop using it and have it checked by an electrician, or throw it away.

Plugs and fuses: Distributors and retailers, including second-hand dealers and auction houses, must only sell appliances that are correctly fitted with an approved plug with sleeved pins and the correct fuse.

Search for Spares Online

From time to time, you will need to buy spares for many electrical items. These spares can include vacuum cleaner bags, bulbs, grill pans and coffee filters, or possibly new knobs or seals for larger appliances. In most cases, you will find better prices online than instore, and it is often possible to get hold of parts for products that have been discontinued for years, or for very obscure brands. Three of the best sites are:

 www.espares.co.uk   **www.spares2go.co.uk**   **www.partmaster.co.uk**

Televisions

Prices have dropped dramatically in recent years and technology is moving at such a cracking pace that flat-screen televisions are now commonplace. It seems that no sooner does a new television come out than it is superseded by the next version, which is great news for bargain hunters as older lines are often sold off cheaply.

TV Buying Tips

Know when and what to buy to find the product you are after for less.

Get Your Timing Right

You will find the best deals in the January and summer sales, and in early summer too. If you are after a new model in time for Christmas, it is best to start shopping well in advance, as this is peak season with fewer reductions.

Select a Popular Size

Competition between dealers is especially fierce on the most popular sizes, so you are more likely to find good deals on televisions with 26 in to 42 in screens.

Go for an Own-Brand Model

You will pay less for own-brand TVs – such as Matsui from Currys and Dixons – than for big-name brands, without compromising on quality.

Double Up

If you are after a DVD player as well as a television, double up with a TV-DVD 'combi' which costs less than buying two separate products.

Opt for a Digital Upgrade

We are all going digital over the next few years and once the switchover happens, analogue televisions will cease to work. But rather than throwing yours away, upgrade to digital viewing by means of a digital box, satellite dish or cable TV, all of which cost a fraction of the price of a new television.

Look Out for the Digital Tick

Televisions with a digital tick logo have been designed to work after the switchover, so it is a false economy to buy a model without the logo, however cheap it is.

Formats

By far the most popular format is widescreen, but if you are happy to put up with a standard format – perhaps for a guest bedroom or other room that is only used occasionally – you can make considerable savings. You will also pay less for models that do not incorporate the latest, must-have features, such as High Definition pictures or surround sound.

Do Your Research

You will get the best value for money if your television incorporates all the features you want without you paying extra for ones that you will not use. Research prices and features online and in-store, and once you have narrowed down your hunt, look into where you can get the best deal.

DVD Players and Recorders, CDs, DVDs and Other Electricals

Technology has moved on quickly in this area too, and you will find anything from basic, entry-level DVD players through to state-of-the-art Blu-ray disc players, which are compatible with regular DVDs. For recording programmes, choose either a standard or a hard drive recorder.

Buying Tips

Choose an Obsolete Model

High Definition DVD players are no longer being made, as they have been outclassed by Blu-ray technology. They are compatible with HD-TVs and can be found on sale at very competitive prices.

Buy the Right Recorder

Hard disc recorders cost more than standard models but give you greater flexibility as they store large quantities of films, photos and other data, and reduce the need to keep buying blank DVDs.

Find a Region-Free DVD Player

As far as DVDs are concerned, the world is divided into regions and if your DVD player is 'locked' you will only be able to play discs which have been released in that zone – usually Europe or the USA. A region-free DVD player enables you to play all DVDs, regardless of where they come from, and gives you access to cheaper prices when buying abroad.

Where to Get the Best Deals

Choice and price variations are so huge that it is vital to do your homework to ensure you get the best deals.

Check Out Price Comparison Websites

Visit www.pricerunner.co.uk and www.kelkoo.co.uk to find where big brand names are being sold for less.

High Street and Department Stores

The advantage of shopping in-store is that you get to see the picture and sound quality, and try models out for yourself. There are frequent special offers on TVs, DVD players and recorders, both in-store and online, but you need to snap them up quickly. Again, John Lewis comes up trumps here, with low prices and a free five-year guarantee on all televisions, which few other stores and companies can match. Stores have large ranges in stock, so you should be able to take your purchase with you, or free delivery is offered, as preferred.

Supermarkets

Shop in a large supermarket and chances are you will find reasonably-priced televisions and DVD players in the aisles, alongside packets of coffee and cereal. These products are normally placed near the entrance to grab customers as they step through the door. Before snapping one up, take time to consider whether it has the features you want, or whether you are simply seduced by the price. And, as you are unlikely to have the chance to try it out, remember to check that it can be returned if you are not happy with it.

Electrical Superstores

Bulk buys ensure low prices and plenty of choice, so visit a superstore to get an idea of what is out there and the prices you are likely pay. Get staff to demonstrate products and never feel under obligation to buy. And it is always worth asking whether display or demonstration models are for sale, with extra reductions, of course.

Specialist Electrical Outlets

For expert advice and to get all your questions answered, visit a specialist store such as Maplins, www.maplins.com, or Richer Sounds, www.richersounds.com. Check out their websites for keenly priced sale and clearance bargains.

Online

Hundreds of online companies sell discounted televisions, DVD players and recorders, but the site offering the lowest price on one model will not necessarily be the cheapest for another. The following sites are always well worth visiting:

- www.amazon.co.uk
- www.play.com
- www.digitaldirect.co.uk
- www.comet.co.uk
- www.laskys.com
- www.hugesdirect.co.uk

Second-Hand Bargains

Unlike kitchen appliances, which many of us keep until they start to go wrong, there is a fast turnover in second-hand televisions, as people often like to upgrade to the latest model. Try eBay, Gumtree and www.teleland.co.uk for second-hand and reconditioned models, and remember to check them for electrical safety.

Save on CDs and DVDs

There are many ways you can buy discounted CDs and DVDs, but keep well clear of pirate DVDs and websites that let you download pirated music.

 Online: The internet is nearly always cheaper than the high street – try www.amazon.co.uk, www.play.com and www.101cd.com for a wide range of music and films.

✓ **Rent:** Hiring a film costs less than buying, so join an online film club such as www.blockbuster.co.uk or www.lovefilm.com and enjoy introductory offers usually in the form of free films – and unlimited rentals. If you prefer to build up a movie collection, find pre-owned DVDs for less at www.dvd4music.com, or bid for them on eBay.

✓ **iTunes:** And rather than forking out for a pricey CD, the advent of iTunes means that music fans only have to pay for tracks they like.

Other Electricals

From cameras, camcorders and game consoles to DAB digital radios and MP3 players, there is no reason why you should have to pay full price on any electrical items. Always research items carefully, compare prices online and in-store, and ask whether any extras will be included in the price.

Computers

A drop in prices combined with increased reliance on the internet means that few homes now manage without a computer. Thanks to frequent upgrades and technological advances, there is never a shortage of bargains, as retailers want to shift old stock to make room for the latest models. Decent discounts are available on most major brands of PC, but it is rare to find reductions on current Apple Macs products.

Buying Tips

You will find the best discounts when excitement over a new model or software upgrade has dimmed, so be prepared to play the waiting game to make higher savings.

Check Specs

Check specifications carefully as slight variations can make big differences in price.

Assess Your Hard Drive Requirements

You will pay more for additional hard drive space – 100 GB is sufficient for most people, though you will need more if you wish to store large quantities of images or movies.

Desktops v. Laptops

Laptops or more compact notebooks tend to cost slightly more than their desktop equivalents, though prices are levelling out.

Consider Returns

There are often big savings on new computers which have been returned, unused, to the manufacturer. But avoid used computers as even if the data has been wiped, they may run slowly or even be corrupted.

Buy a Bundle

Ask the dealer to put together a bundle of hardware and software, either thrown in for free or at a price far lower than the individual components.

Where to Buy

The net generally offers better bargains, but you might get lucky on the high street. Shop around as prices vary considerably, but sites and stores which consistently offer low prices include PC World, www.pcworld.co.uk. Try also: www.it247.com and www.computerbargains.co.uk.

Printers, Scanners and Other Accessories

Literally dozens of accessories and peripherals are available to help you get the most from your PC. These are the ones you will almost certainly need – you can buy them alongside your computer, or possibly find them cheaper elsewhere.

Printer

Haggle for a bulk discount if you buy your printer at the same time as your PC. An inexpensive inkjet printer will suffice if you plan to print only documents, but paying slightly more for a photo printer means you can print your own digital photos, saving money on getting this done in-store. Remember to find out how much ink cartridges cost, as they vary tremendously in price.

All-In-One Printer

If you need a scanner as well as a printer, your best bet is to buy an all-in-one that incorporates a copier as well – and is less expensive than buying separate products.

Blank Discs

Own-brand discs cost less than branded ones, so use these if you burn a lot of material. Unless you reuse discs again and again, buy cheaper CD-Rs or DVD-Rs rather than CDs and DVD-RWs.

Ink

Ink cartridges can be a significant running expense if you print a lot of documents or photos. Cut costs by trying compatible, unbranded rather than branded cartridges, which can be half the price. Various online companies offer good deals, particularly if you are buying several cartridges at a time. Try www.cartridgesave.co.uk, www.365ink.co.uk, www.printcartridgedirect.com, or reuse empty cartridges by getting them refilled at a branch of Cartridge World, www.cartridgeworld.org.

Software

Basic software is usually included with your computer, but additional security and spreadsheet software can be costly, although students and teachers may be entitled to academic discounts. But there are certain downloads that everyone can get for free. Log on to www.free.grisoft.com for the effective AVG antivirus programme, or get OpenOffice, similar in many ways to Microsoft Office, free at www.openoffice.org. And download Firefox, an excellent browser, at www.mozilla.com/en-US/firefox.

Clothes & Accessories

High Street

You might think the high street is the last place to go for bargains as the price you see is often the price you pay. But there are many ways to sniff out a good deal and as credit crunch-hit retailers vie for your custom you may be surprised how flexible they can be. This section shows you how to handle the seasonal sales, scope out the best discount retailers on the high street and manage the store card minefield. We also give you tips on shopping for second-hand clothes, finding sample sales and mastering the art of haggling.

High Street Tips

Price Match

Not all high-street stores are willing to price match with online retailers because prices are typically a lot less, but it is always worth asking. If they lower their price by a reasonable amount, consider whether the postage you would pay if you bought the same item online makes the offer worthwhile.

Shop in the Kids' Section

This tip won't work for everyone, but if you wear small sizes check children's departments for things like T-shirts and vests. Sometimes shoes in children's shops go up to a size four or five, which will fit some women, although of course you are unlikely to find bargain stiletto heels! Kidswear is exempt from VAT so if you can find and fit into styles you like you can make big savings.

Buy Out of Season

This takes some forward planning, but if you stock up your wardrobe for the following season during the sales you could save a fortune.

Store Cards

The big department stores such as Debenhams and House of Fraser all have store card schemes and many other chain stores now have them too including Topshop, Oasis and River Island. They should be used with extreme caution because the interest rates are usually sky-high – APRs can be up to 30 per cent. But if you pay off the balance in full each time you

use them you can take advantage of introductory offers such as 10 per cent off purchases and receive invitations to sale previews so you can bag the best bargains.

Sales

Some shoppers stock their whole wardrobes for the year by getting up at the crack of dawn to hit the January sales. The thought of joining the hordes camping outside Next the night before Boxing Day might fill you with horror, but thankfully this is not the only way to get the best from the sales.

Look For The Red Dot

Scope out your favourite shop a few days before its seasonal sale begins. Items that are going to be marked down will often have a red or black dot on the price tag or on the label inside the garment.

Ask Shop Assistants

Sales staff will know which items are going to be reduced in upcoming sales. If you are considering buying something at full price first ask whether it will be reduced and by how much. Then make sure you come back early on the first day of the sale before your item is snapped up by another shopper.

Stay Focused

It is easy to get distracted by large markdowns at sale time. Make sure you have a clear idea of exactly what you want in order to avoid being seduced by supposed bargains. Don't go into a shop looking for a black sweater and come out with a pair of lime green hot pants just because they had 70 per cent off.

Leave It to the Last Minute

Arriving early is generally a good strategy for getting the most out of seasonal sales. But another riskier plan is to leave it until the last few days before a sale finishes, when many unsold items are either reduced further or offered as buy-one-get-one-free or three-for-two. You will tend to find the things left are the least common sizes, or perhaps shop-soiled, but remember you can get things altered to fit quite cheaply. Similarly, unravelling hems are easy to fix and make-up stains from where things have been tried on can be erased with stain remover in your wash.

Discount Retailers

Even the most snooty fashionistas have embraced stores like Primark as a way to find on-trend clothes and accessories at impossibly low prices. But a £2 T-shirt actually has a much higher cost, both human and environmental. Although Primark claims to have rectified the problems it had with sweatshops in its supply chain, the environmental impact of so much slow degrading textile waste ending up in landfills could be disastrous. For those unwilling to boycott these kinds of stores completely, it is perhaps more eco-conscious to buy quality wardrobe staples from more expensive retailers and use discount shops for seasonal items you will wear less frequently. Work out the cost per wear of key pieces such as a well made suit and you will see that shopping exclusively at pile-it-high, sell-it-cheap retailers can be a false economy.

Matalan

This discount chain operates from out of town sites to save on overheads, passing these savings on to customers. It does require a membership but this is free and you can get a card instantly in store. Matalan sells branded jeans such as Lee and Wrangler, and underwear such as Wonderbra and Sloggi at large discounts. It also has a huge range of its own-brand clothes, shoes and accessories. It is especially good for childrenswear and basics like T-shirts, vests, hosiery, socks and boxer shorts.

Primark

Primark sells its own-brand products, including bra and knicker sets from £4, vest tops from £2 and dresses for around £8. It also has a huge range of accessories and a growing selection of footwear. Its range consists primarily of simply designed clothing in unfussy fabrics and it does not advertise, which helps keep costs down.

TK Maxx

TK Maxx stocks remaindered, returned and end-of-line products from well-known labels at a 50 or 60 per cent discount. This chain store has grown in popularity and can now be found on most high streets in the UK.

Supermarkets

Smart shoppers should not overlook supermarkets for excellent deals on clothing alongside your weekly food shop. Asda has the George range and Tesco has Florence & Fred, both of which will be available online in the near future.

School Uniforms

Supermarket ranges are especially good for mums on a budget as their school uniform ranges are typically very cheap. This might be one instance where it is sensible to buy cheap clothes rather than high quality ones because most kids will have outgrown them in less than a year anyway.

Loyalty Schemes

Tesco's Clubcard loyalty scheme allows customers to collect points when they spend in-store, which are then converted to money-off vouchers. Points can be earned and vouchers spent on its clothing range as well as on groceries.

Sales and Clearance Shops

Many high street retailers have dedicated sale or clearance stores for their end-of-line or old season stock. A cursory check using a search engine should bring up a list of these in your area.

High Street Clearance Stores

Office, for example, has various sale shops around the country offering heavily discounted shoes. Sometimes items are shop-soiled but generally they are simply old stock priced to clear. Next Clearance Stores sell previous seasons' stock at a lower price than the core Next branches.

Designer Outlets

These are out of town shopping centres through which manufacturers sell direct to the public with up to 70 per cent reductions. Check www.shoppingvillage.com for details of your nearest outlet. Bear in mind that due to the sites on which they operate, they are often most easily accessed by car.

Sample Sales

Keep an eye on the local press and websites, such as Time Out, for advance warning of designer sample sales. You can also sign up to free site such as www.secretsales.com to get access to closed sample sales from labels including Versace, Replay and Diesel. Membership is

limited – once it closes you can only join by referral – and returns are allowed but you have to pay for postage. Others include www.catwalktocloset.com and www.dailycandy.com which covers the US and the UK and recently offered access to discounted Vera Wang wedding dresses.

Discounts

You don't have to remind most hard-up students to make the most of their NUS card, but many shops will accept other proof you are studying such as international student cards or even library cards, often at the sales assistant's discretion. Another option is staff discount schemes which are often extremely generous in high street stores so it pays to use your contacts.

Work Discount Schemes

Some employers have schemes in place for staff to get discounts from local businesses. If yours doesn't have one, ask if it is possible to set one up. For example, workers in the West End of London have access to the WOW Privilege Card scheme, which offers a discount at Gap. The larger your company, the easier it should be to negotiate with local retailers. Businesswear suppliers often have discount schemes with offices – shirtmaker TM Lewin says members of its discount scheme pay less than half price in stores and can also claim reduced prices online.

Haggling

As a general rule, you have more chance of haggling successfully the more you are spending. Ask for a discount if you're buying several items, or see if the retailer will throw an accessory in for free. Shops often reward regular customers with price reductions or freebies. Ask politely with a smile and you might be surprised what you can get.

Second-Hand

'Pre-loved' clothes have had something of a revival as discerning shoppers become more ecologically aware and rein in their spending as inflation rises. If you don't want to walk around town wearing the same outfit as everyone else, second-hand clothes can help you create a unique look.

Vintage

Not only are they comparatively cheaper, vintage clothes tend to be higher quality than much of the disposable fashion around today. You will pay more in chains like London's Rokit than if you go to street markets. Girls can make it easier to try things on when shopping at markets by wearing leggings and a vest under your clothes so you can change in public without embarrassment. It always makes sense to try things on because sizing on vintage clothes rarely corresponds to modern sizes. Remember alterations can make a fabulous find into a tailor-made perfect fit for very little money. And don't forget to haggle.

Pawn Shops

Sadly these have had something of a revival as more people suffer the effects of the credit crunch. Pawnbrokers make high interest loans, lending against something the borrower leaves

behind as collateral. If the borrower cannot repay the loan in the agreed timescale, the broker sells the item. Pawn shops can be excellent places to find good quality second-hand jewellery or pricier items of clothing like leather jackets.

Charity Shops

Charity shops can turn up some excellent finds if you are prepared to spend a bit of time rummaging. Go to shops in affluent neighbourhoods to increase your chances of finding second-hand designer threads. In London, Kensington, Chelsea and Notting Hill boast a wealth (pardon the pun) of shops selling cast-off Jean Paul Gaultier, Vivienne Westwood and Gucci. The Red Cross on Old Church Street in Chelsea only stocks designer labels – Manolo Blahnik sometimes drops off donations.

Jumble Sales and Car Boot Sales

Flea markets, jumble sales and car boot sales require a bit of effort but can be a fun day out as well as saving you money. Look for sales near student digs towards the end of term when those who blew their loan in Topshop in freshers' week are trying to recoup it by selling clothes off cheap. Of course, haggling is par for the course. Sellers are often having a wardrobe clear-out and are happy to accept reasonable offers. You have to get up very early to make the most of car boots – sellers will be setting up their pitches at 6 a.m. and professionals get there early to grab the best items for resale. Try www.carbootjunction.com or your local press for listings of upcoming events in your area. And make sure you take a raincoat – inclement weather is definitely a feature of UK car boot sales.

Online

Thrifty shopping on the web can be a daunting task with such a vast array of retailers competing for your attention. This section covers eBay as well as some lesser known auction sites, how to get access to secret designer sample sales and tips for making exchange rates work for you by buying from abroad. It also helps you track down discounts and vouchers and tells you how you can get paid for shopping with mainstream online retailers. You can also learn how to find freebies on the net, make price comparison sites work to your advantage and use community forums to downsize your clothing spend.

Auction Websites

eBay is the UK's largest and most well-known auction site, but it has come under fire lately for allowing major retailers such as Argos, Littlewoods and Schuh to list items for instant sale at fixed prices. Buyers have shown a preference for this format and this has led to a drop in sales for smaller, independent sellers. Many have returned to their pre-eBay activities in the belief that eBay is no longer a collectors' market. For buyers who are finding it harder to get good deals on unusual items these days, it might be worth checking out some of the many other comparable sites. See www.auctionlotwatch.co.uk for a comprehensive list of UK auctions, including some specialist jewellery and vintage sites.

Know What You Are Bidding For

One of the best ways to save money on eBay is to make sure you know that the item you are bidding for is exactly what you want and will fit you. Don't be afraid to ask the seller questions to clarify details, especially if the photo is unclear or does not include measurements of the

garment. If you do buy something that turns out to be the wrong size or otherwise unsuitable, why not put it back on eBay and resell it? You may even earn more than you paid for it in the first place.

Sniping

This is when you watch an item in My eBay but don't place a bid until the last possible second so other bidders have no time to counter-bid. Never bid on something you want early on in the auction as you will only drive up the price as others try to outbid you. Make sure you check Completed Listings to get an idea of the going rate and avoid getting carried away in a bidding war and paying too much. There are tools to snipe for you, but most involve a charge for each auction won, or a monthly subscription, except www.goofbay.com which is free. Both www.ezsniper.com and www.auctionsniper.com offer a free trial – just be sure you cancel in time to avoid being charged.

Postage

Where possible, set your own postage charge – check Royal Mail's website to find out what it should cost. Query postage charges you think are too high as some sellers use them as a way to make additional profit. You can also search for items closest to your location so you can collect goods in person where the seller allows.

Best Offer

Some eBay shops give you the option to make a Best Offer. Use the Advanced Search option to find the item you want, selecting the Best Offer box. Then use View Seller's Other Items followed by Completed Listings to check what similar items have sold for. You can then make an offer slightly below and with any luck the seller will accept. This trick works better in eBay shops than with individual sellers because shops buy in bulk and will typically sell several of the same item.

Alerts

eBay has an email alert system to let you know when something you are looking for is listed. To set up a new alert, go to the All Favourites link in My eBay and select Searches. You then have the option to specify exactly what you want, its location and even items with few or no bids. You can save time as well as money doing this as you could spend hours trawling the site for new listings.

Grab a Bargain

Check the Grab a Bargain section for auctions closing soon, but have a clear idea in mind of what you want to buy to avoid being seduced by cheap things you don't really need. Use www.auctionfinal.com to scour listings ending soon.

Misspelling

Misspell words when you're searching for listings – you can find real gems that might otherwise go undiscovered because of a simple typo. eBay's own search engine only identifies actual words, so make the most of the various free tools that will pick up misspelled listings for you. These include www.fatfingers.com, www.missingauctions.co.uk and www.goofbay.com.

International Sellers

Use eBay's Advanced Search tool to check if an item you want is available from an international seller, or visit eBay.com to compare US prices. This search engine can also find items by location and even currency. Remember to take shipping charges and possible customs tax into account when bidding (see the section on Buying from Abroad, page 70, for more details on this).

Take a Chance

Many people won't buy from new sellers with low feedback scores (note, this is different from people with negative feedback, who you should avoid), or listings with no photo and a very brief description. You can find bargains this way if you're willing to take the risk, but it is not advisable for high value items.

Marketplaces and Freebies

Contrary to popular belief, it is possible to get something for nothing if you know where to look.

Gumtree and Craigslist

Community websites www.gumtree.com and www.craigslist.org both have freebies sections where you can occasionally find clothes and accessories being given away. You are almost always expected to go and pick items up in person. The best things go quickly so don't hesitate if you see something you like. These sites are often a good bet for children's clothes that have been outgrown. Otherwise both sites have marketplaces where you can buy second-hand clothes. Sellers usually accept reasonable offers. Social networking site Facebook also has a burgeoning marketplace section, and you can also create your own Items Wanted post and let the bargains come to you.

Freecycle

This not-for-profit organisation – www.freecycle.org – is structured as a global network run through local Yahoo online groups. It encourages users to give away unwanted goods to those who need them, strengthening community ties and reducing landfill. It currently has over four million members worldwide. Members sign up to receive email alerts when new things are listed and they arrange collection with the giver. You can also post requests for things you want. Freecycle emphasizes it is not simply a place to come to find free stuff – it encourages members to offer something of their own to the community first.

Price Comparison Websites

Using these websites is much quicker and easier than spending hours searching the web trying to find the best price for a specific item. They make their money either on a pay-per-click basis or by taking a small cut of sales made via the site. It is sensible to check several of the larger ones to ensure you cast your net wide enough across a range of different retailers. Avoid those with affiliations to particular shops and go to the unbiased sites for the best recommendations. It is also worth checking if postage is included in the price quoted. If you are buying more than one item from the same retailer you can often pay less for postage. The best sites will also give you estimated lead times for delivery – useful if you need something in a hurry. See also chapter one in this book, which is all about these websites in general.

UK Sites

The most well-known ones in the UK are www.pricerunner.co.uk, www.kelkoo.co.uk, www.uk.shopping.com and www.shopzilla.co.uk. Many of the major internet search engines now also have separate shopping comparison tools, including MSN, Yahoo, Google and AOL.

US Sites

Popular US comparison sites include www.aimlower.com, www.pricecomparison.com and www.smarter.com.

Discounts and Rebates

Many sites have a dedicated section for rebates, money-off vouchers and discount codes offered by retailers exclusively to users. Check the expiry dates on these offers to ensure you don't miss out – sometimes they have a short shelf life.

Online Discounts

There are many sources of vouchers and discount codes to be found on the web as well as cashback sites that actually pay you to shop online.

Cashback Websites

Sites such as www.quidco.com, www.cashbackjunction.com or www.pigsback.com register you so that when you use a link through the cashback site to buy from a range of retailers, your click-through is logged. Then the retailer gives you cashback in the form of a percentage of your spend or a flat fee. The site takes a cut of any cashback you earn and the rest is paid regularly into your bank account. Quidco takes the first £5 of anything you make annually, but if you don't earn anything in the course of a year you will not be charged. Fashion retailers linked to Quidco include Debenhams, Burtons, Office and Boden.

Forums and Newsletters

Forums are your friend – they are an excellent free resource for thrifty shoppers. Martin Lewis's www.moneysavingexpert.com has a tool to help you find which cashback site pays the most for purchases from your chosen retailer. It also has a section on its message boards for up-to-date discount codes and a free e-newsletter which includes the best deals each week. Try www.ukfrenzy.co.uk or www.cantBarsed.com for discount codes. Fashion site www.handbag.com's newsletter often includes promotions and special discounts. In the US, www.totallyfrugal.com and www.fatwallet.com can help you find the best offers.

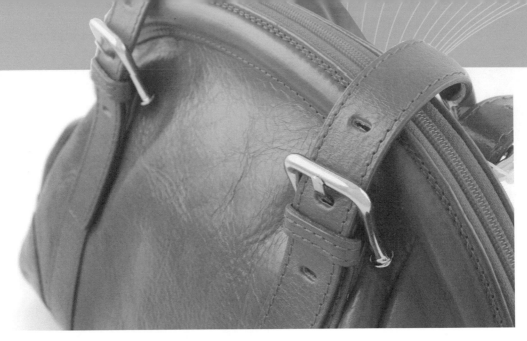

Shop Internationally Online

If you feel you can offset your carbon footprint, take advantage of the weak dollar while you can by buying from the US. Many online retailers will ship overseas and you can save a packet as long as you take into account shipping costs and any charges you might incur as your goods pass through customs. Big brand clothing retailers that do ship to the UK include Doc Martens, Victoria's Secret, JC Penney and LL Bean.

Shipping

If you are buying more than one item, try to negotiate on postage costs to make sure you really are getting value for money. If you want to buy from a site that will not ship to the UK, you could consider using a mail forwarding service such as www.mailforwarding.biz or www.myus.com. Of course, delivery lead times may also vary and sending something using fast delivery could end up costing you a lot more.

Customs

Money Saving Expert recommends adding 30 per cent to the US price of an item to cover delivery, customs charges and VAT. Of course this is a rough guide so you should check with the seller exactly what the final price will be before committing to buy.

Currency Conversion

If you have the option to pay in pounds don't take it – there's no guarantee the exchange rate will be favourable and the retailer may take a cut from the conversion.

Online-Only Retailers

Budget fashion doesn't have to be, well, unfashionable! Several websites have sprung up offering very affordable clothes and accessories that mirror the hottest designers' creations. These companies don't have a presence on the high street so they are able to pass their lower operating costs on to their customers.

Asos

Asos (short for As Seen On Screen), at www.asos.com, makes convincing copies of outfits worn by celebrities including Lindsay Lohan, Mary Kate Olsen and Cameron Diaz and sells them for a fraction of the price. Asos has recently started offering a wider range of clothing including pricier labels such as Miss Sixty, All Saints and Lipsy, but there are still good value own-brand items to be had.

Boohoo

www.boohoo.com offers very competitive pricing although the quality of goods can vary. It charges reasonable postage and, unlike similar sites, offers free returns making it even better value.

Buy Copies

This does not mean illegal counterfeit goods but decent copies of designer handbags that don't actually rip off the original. Try www.mypursemall.com for 'designer inspired replicas'. If you are desperate for an original, there are sites that import handbags, purses and watches from overseas giving you hefty savings on the genuine article. At the time of writing, www.bagnificent.co.uk had Balenciaga bags at a £430 discount to the recommended price and www.koodos.com had Chloe quilted bowling bags with 35 per cent off.

More Top Fashion Tips

There are many ways you can cut down the amount you spend on looking fashionable if you think creatively. Hiring expensive suits, dresses or accessories can work out much cheaper than forking out hundreds of pounds to own them. This section also tackles catalogue shopping which can be a great money saver for disciplined shoppers. Getting clothing made to measure or bespoke from scratch can be a brilliant alternative to disposable fashion and may not cost as much as you think. Going abroad for good deals on clothes is also an option. Finally, we look at savings on hair and beauty.

Hire

An option that deserves a mention is hiring outfits rather than buying them outright. Tuxedos, ball gowns and Halloween costumes are the mainstay of many clothing agencies, but often you can also hire jewellery, handbags, shoes and even kilts.

Clothing Hire

Hiring occasion wear may seem pricey but if you work out the cost per wear of a brand new item like an evening gown or a dress suit, you may find it is the cheaper option. It also means you can afford to have a fresh look for every formal event you attend. This applies especially to hats and fascinators which can really make a statement. It is advisable to shop around and compare prices for hiring an item like a dinner suit which is unlikely to vary much in style – start with www.freeindex.co.uk which has a decent list of clothing hire businesses in the UK.

Rent Handbags

Sites are springing up offering fashionistas on a budget the chance to have the hottest designer handbag for as long as they want. For a monthly fee you can rotate items as often as you want, although there may be additional charges for couture or vintage items. If you are concerned you might subject your borrowed bag to a bit too much wear, you can purchase optional insurance in case of damage. Some companies allow you to purchase any item you borrow and then fall in love with, working out the cost based on its age and condition. Often you can also hire sunglasses and other accessories. Try www.be-a-fashionista.co.uk in the UK or www.bagborroworsteal.com in the US.

Overseas Shopping Trips

Goodies can be had for cheaper prices abroad and flights are cheaper than ever with more budget airlines breaking on to the scene – although with the price of fuel on the rise this trend could be short-lived. Don't forget to bring an empty suitcase to haul your goodies back home.

New York: A hugely popular destination for Christmas shopping trips and with the dollar weak against sterling and the euro, there has never been a better time to go.

Milan: A premier destination for designer clothes but, although the choice will be wider, you are unlikely to save as much on the big labels as you might elsewhere.

Moscow, Stockholm and Johannesburg: These are all beginning to blossom as fashion capitals.

Stay in the UK: However, consider the environment before you jet off to Dubai's shopping district on a whim. If you would rather cut your carbon footprint you could visit some of the UK's best shopping cities, including London, Glasgow, Manchester and Bristol.

Check Allowances

UK customs rules allow you to bring up to £145 worth of goods including souvenirs into the country from outside the EU. There is no limit on goods bought within the EU.

Duty-free

The first things you associate with duty-free shops might be booze and cigarettes, but you can also make great savings on bags, wallets, purses, watches and jewellery. Duty-free shopping has not been allowed for travellers within the EU for several years but if your destination is further afield you can still take advantage of tax-free prices.

Catalogue Shopping

Buying from catalogues is not just for bored housewives. Shopping by mail order can be dangerous if you lack discipline, but if you are canny and armed with all the facts you can take advantage of discounts and flexible payment plans. Treat catalogue accounts with the same degree of caution as store cards and you could benefit from substantial savings.

Postage

Many catalogue companies offer free postage and returns, so you can try things on in the comfort of your own home and avoid the hordes on the high street. Be sure to store things carefully at home before you return them to avoid being charged for damage.

Instalments

You can normally spread the cost of purchases by paying in instalments, but this can often attract a hefty interest rate. Freemans and Kays both charge 29.9 per cent APR if you do not pay off your account balance in full every month. There are often interest-free periods of up to two years, but they can apply only to certain purchases, so make sure you check the fine print very carefully.

Initial Discounts

Most catalogues offer a discount off your first purchase, often between 10 and 20 per cent, so wait until you need several items and buy in one go. Then you should pay off the balance in full and close the account to escape the astronomical interest.

Bespoke and Made-to-Measure Clothing

Having quality pieces tailor-made to fit you is a really good investment and it doesn't have to cost an arm and a leg.

Dressmakers

Imagine you see a gorgeous dress you really want but it costs a fortune. Try it on, take a couple of snaps on your mobile phone of you wearing it, then visit fabric stockists for similar material. Shops in Indian or Chinese districts are good for this as they often have beautiful fabric at very reasonable prices. Write down your measurements and take your photos and fabric to a dressmaker. Use the Yellow Pages or ask friends for recommendations. It costs much less than you think and you will end up with a made to measure outfit you will be more likely to wear again. You can even do the whole process online at www.styleshake.com.

Tailors

Find a good tailor to custom-make or alter your businesswear – spending more on one or two high quality, well-fitting suits is a good investment. A bespoke garment is one made to your exact specifications without the use of a pre-existing pattern, while made to measure means a basic pattern is altered to fit your measurements. As you might expect, bespoke suits will cost quite a bit more. You don't have to go to Savile Row for services like these – www.freeindex.co.uk lists tailors throughout the UK.

Make-Up

Decent make-up and skincare can cost a small fortune, but you don't have to overpay if you know where to look. Online retailer Eyes Lips Face (ELF) stocks modern and stylish make-up at ridiculously low prices, and has UK and US websites.

Tester Websites

These sites post you samples of products to try in exchange for your feedback, usually through a short questionnaire. Recently launched www.latestinbeauty.com lets you sign up to try brand new make-up, skincare products and perfumes before they hit the market, charging £1 for postage on three samples at a time.

Makeovers

Get free makeovers at the make-up counters in department stores and places like Boots. Book in before a night out, but make sure you have baby wipes with you in case of disaster – some make-up counter girls can be a little overzealous!

Free Samples

Testers from make-up counters in department stores can add a bit of glamour to your make-up bag for free. Say you're thinking of overhauling your skincare regime or replacing all your old, tired make-up. If the sales assistant thinks you are potentially a big spender they should lavish you with free samples. Just try to avoid being drawn into expensive purchases by the hard sell that will inevitably follow. There are also many websites offering free cosmetics and money-off vouchers – check www.healthandbeautyfreebies.co.uk.

Hair and Beauty

Not strictly clothing, but what's the point of wearing your new bargain outfit if your hair is all over the place? Professional haircuts are expensive for both men and women, but if you are time-rich and cash-poor there are options to help you cut the cost and still look good.

Modelling

Toni and Guy, Michael John and Vidal Sassoon all have academies offering free or heavily discounted cuts and colours in exchange for using you as a guinea pig for trainees. Local salons and beauty schools also need models to try out experimental styles. You need patience though – a cut and colour can take up to three hours. Junior stylists are supervised so the potential for

disaster is minimal, but there are no guarantees you will like the finished look. Check www.gumtree.com, community message boards or salon windows for adverts. For beauty treatments, the London School of Beauty has a student salon called Esthetique offering a wide range of treatments for less than half the price you would normally pay.

Loyalty Schemes

If you regularly use the same hair or beauty salon find out whether they have a loyalty card scheme in place, or if not, whether they could start one. They work along the same lines as schemes coffee shops use – you get a stamp each time you go and then a free or reduced cut when you have notched up several visits.

Travel

Cars

Spiralling fuel prices have left many car owners facing bigger bills for travelling in their own vehicles. But there are plenty of other ways you can cut down on motoring costs, such as getting the lowest price for insurance, petrol and breakdown cover. The secret is knowing where to look.

Insurance

When it comes to insuring your vehicle, it pays to roll your sleeves up and do some research. Simply renewing your deal with your existing insurer is likely to eat up more of your budget than necessary, as many insurers offer enticing deals for new customers in a bid to increase their business.

Price Comparison Websites for Insurance

There are some top-notch comparison websites to help you start the search. If you don't have internet access at home (and check the next chapter to make sure you aren't paying over the odds if you do) it may even be worth paying to go to an internet café to kick off your search for the cheapest insurance deal.

- **Websites:** Some of the main comparison sites for car insurance are www.confused.com, www.gocompare.com and www.moneysupermarket.com. You can enter your details in these sites and they will retrieve quotes from a wide range of insurers. A couple of minutes on the websites will save you hours on the phone.

- **Visit more than one:** But it is always worth visiting more than one comparison site, whatever type of insurance or cover you are looking for, as sites may have different panels of insurers on their books. Direct Line, one of the leading insurers in the UK, does not work with these websites, so it might be worth calling them separately.

Call direct: Also, not all insurers offer their best deals via the internet, so once you are armed with some of the most competitive quotes it is time to hit the phone and call the insurers that offer the most competitive quotes directly and see if you can cut your premiums further.

Haggle With Your Insurer

When you ring up an insurer about a policy, don't be afraid to let them know you have researched the market and what deals you can get with their rivals. You might be surprised what they are able to offer. Before you sign on the dotted line, you might like to try giving your current insurer a call. Tell them what the new insurer is offering and you may well find that they are persuaded to drop the renewal price. In other words, don't reserve haggling for buying carpets on your holidays!

Try Some 'Quote Massaging'

Insurers take your job into account when they give you a quote for car cover. So do try different ways of describing your job to see if it makes a difference – it could cut your premium by tens or hundreds of pounds a year. Experts call this 'quote massaging.' For instance, a solicitor can also be described as a lawyer, while a landlord can also be called a publican. Some insurers have already taken action to make sure all their quotes agree, but do double-check to make sure you are not paying more than you need to.

Exploit Existing Relationships

Another trick when it comes to car insurance is using your existing relationships. Ring your home insurer and ask if they will consider insuring your car. Many insurers are often keen to expand their customer base, so you may be offered an attractive rate.

Make Your Car Thief-Repellent

Not everyone has a lockable garage in which to keep their car, but just as installing a burglar alarm can cut your home insurance premiums, investing in an immobiliser if your car doesn't already have one could cut the cost of cover, especially if you leave your car parked on the street.

Claim Carefully

Most insurers operate a no-claims bonus discount – meaning that drivers who make no claims can expect cheaper insurance cover. A five-year no-claims bonus can entitle drivers to discounts of up to 65 per cent, and in some cases 75 per cent off their premiums with some insurers. If you make a claim, this discount will usually be reduced to an average of around 40 per cent, although the precise discount depends on which insurer you are with. So if you are involved in a minor accident and need to pay out some money, you should carefully weigh up whether it might be worth paying yourself rather than making a claim from your insurer to protect your no-claims bonus. One way to do this is to revisit some comparison sites and type in your details with and without the claim on your record in order to get an idea of what your premium might rise to if you submit a claim.

Insurance for Young Drivers

Use your Parents

If you are a young driver and have your own car, you could be facing sky-high costs for insurance. Typically, the older you are and the less powerful your car, the cheaper your premiums. But one way you can save on insurance costs is to name one of your parents as the second named driver on the vehicle, even if they only drive it infrequently. Don't be tempted

to put your parent down as the main driver if they aren't using the car more than you, however. While it might cut your premiums, it could be enough to invalidate any claim you make.

Avoid Sexing Up Your Car

Don't be tempted to 'pimp your ride'. Research has shown that lowering the suspension on a car can boost premiums by £200 while adding a rear spoiler can increase premiums by up to £100 for a 30-year-old Golf driver. If you have modified your car, you must tell your insurer as failing to do so could result in them turning down your claim.

Take More Driving Lessons

Going back to driving school may be the last thing you feel like doing once you have passed your test, but if you complete a Pass Plus driving course, insurers will be more willing to offer you competitive rates, sometimes cutting up to a third off your premiums. The course takes a minimum of six hours and usually costs between £100 and £150 but some local authorities provide discounts of up to 50 per cent. You can find out if your local authority will help foot the bill at www.passplus.org.uk.

Breakdown Cover

Get the Right Quote

You can choose to take out cover for your vehicle, meaning anyone who drives it is covered, or for yourself – so that you can ask for help in any vehicle you drive. The second type of cover is typically more expensive, but could work out cheaper in the long run if you drive several different cars.

Typically, the more basic cover – for instance, roadside assistance, where a recovery vehicle will take you to the nearest garage – is much cheaper than choosing cover which offers all the bells and whistles including visiting your home if your car won't start in the morning. The best sites for comparing the cost of deals are www.moneysupermarket.com and www.Gocompare.com.

Question Your Renewal Fee

When it comes to paying your renewal premium each year, don't be tempted to pay the sum they ask for without checking the competition. Sometimes you may find that your breakdown cover provider, despite thanking you for years of loyal custom in the renewal letter, is actually offering better deals to new customers. If this is the case, demand that your premium be cut to that level. This usually works, and if it doesn't, you can simply take your custom elsewhere.

Check Your Bank Account

High street banks are increasingly offering perks such as free breakdown cover and free travel insurance with their current accounts. Now, these accounts aren't free – they are often referred to as 'packaged accounts' and usually come with a fee each month. For example, Lloyds TSB offers free AA roadside assistance with its silver current account. To qualify for this account, you must pay in at least £500 a month into the account, and pay a monthly fee of £2 for the first three months and £7.95 thereafter. If you choose Lloyds' Premier Current account, which requires you to pay £1,000 into the account each month, as well as a monthly fee of £25, you will get free comprehensive breakdown cover. This not only offers roadside assistance, but home start – which means you can call for help if your car breaks down in the driveway, as well as replacement vehicles if your car is out of action. Natwest offers free breakdown cover from Green Flag with its Advantage Gold account which costs £12.95 a month. For more details on other packaged accounts and the associated free perks, visit www.moneyfacts.co.uk.

Petrol

The cost of oil has spiralled over the last six months, making filling the tank a more expensive process for every driver. If you usually just pop into your local filling station without checking how its prices compare to rivals, you could be paying over the odds. One way to cut your fuel costs is to drive efficiently – this is covered more in *100 Ways to Beat the Credit Crunch*, another book in the series, but to find cheaper deals have a look at the following advice.

Surf the Web Before You Drive

A quick visit to www.petrolprices.com will show you the most competitive petrol and diesel prices in your area. It covers the whole of the UK and lists prices in nearly 10,000 garage forecourts.

Check Out Reward Schemes

Some supermarkets run discounts on petrol for weeks or months at a time. Tesco is currently offering two free litres of petrol for shoppers who spend £80. If Asda is your local store, it could be worth taking out an Asda credit card, as it offers 2p off for every litre of petrol bought at Asda. Shell also offers a credit card, in conjunction with Citi, which pays you three per cent cashback every time you buy fuel at a Shell garage. (It also pays one per cent cashback on all other purchases, regardless of where you shop.)

Flights and Holidays

Flights, trains, car hire, insurance, travel money – these are some of the things we have to pay for before we even get on holiday. You may have to cut back on your holiday expenditure but you can still get away for less than you think.

Booking Flights

Rising fuel prices have sparked debate about whether the era of cheap flights is over. But there are still lots of bargains out there if you know where to look.

Check Out Comparison Websites

Some of the best websites to compare deals include flight brokers such as www.opodo.com, www.ebookers.com and www.expedia.co.uk, and price comparison websites such as www.travelsupermarket.com and www.kayak.com. Even if you are just looking for flights, it can still be worth checking out package holidays as sometimes the price of flights and

accommodation can be cheaper than a return scheduled flight. You don't have to stay in the hotel included in the packaged holiday deal. www.teletext.com often has good last minute holiday deals too.

Consider Your Travel Times

Very early morning and late night flights are often much cheaper than those at more sociable hours, so choosing to travel at these times can cut the cost of travel greatly. But do bear in mind that many trains to airports stop running at night, so you may need to take a coach instead – which could save you more money. Alternatively, the savings on your plane ticket could fund the cost of a taxi! Avoiding weekend flights will also cut the price of your ticket.

Look Out for the Small Print

But there are also tricks you should be wary of when you are booking flights, either through a travel website or the airlines' own sites, as these can boost the cost of what started out as a cheap ticket. Some airlines, such as Ryanair and BMI automatically tick the box for travel insurance when you are booking your flight, which can add about another £10 to the cost of each ticket. These travel policies do not always offer the best value and if you already have a travel policy it is money wasted, so remember to uncheck the box, otherwise you will be paying for cover that you do not need. For advice on getting the best travel insurance deal, see page 184.

Tot Up All the Hidden Costs

Another trick is to go through to the end of the booking process so you can see what the actual total cost is. While the original prices quoted for flights may seem like a bargain, many airlines now

charge for luggage on top of the cost of your ticket. For example, Ryanair charges an extra £24 if you want to check a piece of luggage into the hold on a return flight from London to Barcelona. In many cases, booking a specific seat will also cost extra, which can add up if you are travelling with a family. Flybe charges £12 if you book a seat on a return flight from Belfast to London, rising to £30 if you choose a seat with extra legroom. The increased cost of oil has also prompted many airlines to levy a fuel surcharge for long-haul flights, beefing up the fees and charges. British Airways' £109 fuel surcharge for a flight from London to Los Angeles is included in its quoted price, while Aer Lingus' charge of £93 is added to the cost of the ticket.

Travel Light

Since the trend these days is to charge you for every item of luggage, packing light will often make your ticket cheaper. If you can carry everything you need in a bag that will fit into the overhead locker, you will pay less and spend a lot less time checking in too. This isn't always possible, however, so do try to buy light suitcases and bags, so that even if you cram them full, you will stay under the weight allowance and not be penalised with extra charges for excess luggage.

Check Out Loyalty Schemes

If you fly regularly, especially if you fly with a specific airline, it might be worth making the money you spend on flights work for you by choosing a loyalty credit card. But if you don't pay off your credit card in full each month, approach this plan with caution, as some of these cards do not offer the most competitive interest rates.

- **Citi:** Their Easyjet mastercard gives you £40 in free flights once you spend £250 on the card. You then receive three Easyjet miles for each £1 spent on Easyjet flights, as well as one Easyjet mile for every pound spent on other purchases. An Easyjet mile is equivalent to 1p. You can then redeem these miles against future tickets.

- **Ryanair and BMI:** These both offer flight points on their credit cards.

- **BA and Virgin:** The British Airways American Express card and Virgin Atlantic White and Black cards also allow you to store up points against flights with the airlines each time you use the card.

- **Lloyds:** The Lloyds TSB Airmiles Duo card offers one Airmile for every £10 spent. Airmiles can be redeemed against flights with about 110 airlines including British Airways. Lloyds also offers an Airmiles mortgage, offering 6,000 free Airmiles with each home loan taken out and an extra 50 Airmiles each month. But you should only consider this deal if the rest of the terms of the mortgage deal suit you. There is no point in paying over the odds on your home loan for the sake of some Airmiles.

- **Tesco Clubcard:** If you are a Tesco Clubcard holder, you can also convert your points into Airmiles.

Find out more: For more details on other ways to collect Airmiles to convert into free flights, visit www.airmiles.co.uk. For details on all other cards, visit moneyfacts.co.uk.

Get Cashback on Your Booking

If you fancy getting cold hard cash or Amazon vouchers when you're booking your holiday, rather than flight points, there are several websites which offer cashback. These sites work by refunding you most of the commission they receive from holiday sites for passing on your booking.

Cashback Kings: For example, at www.cashbackkings.com, you can get 7.25 per cent cashback on hotel bookings, 3.5 per cent cashback on package holidays and one per cent cashback on flights booked through www.expedia.co.uk. You can receive the money into your bank account, or receive payment via a PayPal account. If you want to put the cash towards books, music or travel accessories, you can receive the cash in Amazon vouchers. You can also receive cashback on all sorts of other purchases including £20 for opening a savings account at Alliance & Leicester and 1.5 per cent cashback on online purchases from Argos.

More: Other cashback sites include include www.rpoints.com, www.quidco.com and www.greasypalm.co.uk.

Travel Insurance

There are two different types of travel cover – annual policies, which cover you for every trip you take in a year, and single trip policies, which only provide cover for a single holiday. And there are many other factors to take into account to make sure you get the best deal...

Choose Which Type of Policy You Need

If you take more than two holidays a year, it is likely that an annual policy will be cheaper than buying separate policies each time. If you like skiing or snowboarding, you can buy annual cover which includes winter sports. However, if more adventurous pursuits, such as hang

gliding or bungee jumping, are your thing, it is likely you will have to seek out specialist travel cover as many 'plain vanilla' policies do not cover this type of activity. Likewise, if you are taking a gap year, you will have to look for a tailor-made 'backpacker' policy, as annual cover only covers trips of up to a maximum of 30 or 60 days.

Europe v. Worldwide Cover

If you plan to go island hopping in Greece and skiing in France then Europe-wide cover should be sufficient. A Europe-only travel policy is cheaper than a worldwide policy as medical expenses in the USA are higher than most other countries, bumping up the cost of cover. For this reason it is essential that if you do travel to the USA, you have adequate insurance, as if you don't you could be landed with a hefty bill for medical expenses if you fall ill or have an accident while visiting the country.

Go Online

Start your search at www.moneysupermarket.com, www.confused.com or www.defaqto.co.uk to get an idea of the best deals around. If you are travelling with your family, it will usually be cheaper to get insurance for the whole family, rather than for each individual, although you should always double-check how many people the insurer includes in a 'family' policy.

Check the Small Print: Excess

To check the small print is a piece of advice often bandied about, but it can be tough to plough through pages and pages of tiny type that accompany a travel policy.

Firstly, look at the excess payment. This is the sum you will have to pay for any claim you make. Insurers will often offer cheaper deals for 'no-frills' insurance which often includes a larger excess payment, that is, you will cover the first £150 of any claim. If you want to reduce this excess payment, so you only have to pay £50 if you make a claim, for example, the cost of the policy will be higher, but is unlikely to be £100 higher, so if you are worried about the expensive excess, it is worth upgrading.

Check the Small Print: Baggage

Check the baggage cover. If you aren't bothered about losing suitcases full of suncream and bathing costumes then this is not a priority, but if you are going skiing with lots of expensive kit, then this cover is probably crucial. Check how much the policy will pay for your lost luggage and also check how much it provides towards replacing the items should you need to repurchase them at your destination.

Check the Small Print: Medical

Check the medical insurance. Don't be enticed by massive medical insurance allowances, unless you are travelling to the USA. Medical cover of £2 million should be sufficient if you are travelling in Europe. Which?, the consumer body, recommends you have at least £1 million of medical cover in Europe and £2 million in the rest of the world, personal liability cover of at least £1 million and cover for legal expenses, as well as £1,500 baggage cover and £3,000 cancellation cover. For more information, visit www.which.co.uk/advice/getting-the-right-travel-insurance.

Valuables

Some policies will not pay out more than a certain sum for valuables, regardless of their worth. If you are taking an expensive watch or piece of jewellery with you, make sure you can reclaim its total value if it is lost. If there is not enough cover for the full value of the item on your travel policy, then call your household insurer and ask them to include it within your personal possessions cover. This may cost extra, but will be crucial if you lose it.

Keep Cameras and MP3 Players Locked Away

Also, while on holiday, keep all personal items locked in the safe in your room unless you have them with you. Most insurance policies will not pay out for cameras or MP3 players stolen while in a car or left by the pool. Some policies even refuse to cover jewellery, except wedding rings, lost while swimming in a pool.

Check Your Bank Account and Credit Card

Some banks offer free travel insurance with their packaged or fee-based accounts so, if you already have one of these accounts, there is no point in paying twice. For example, Lloyds TSB offers free annual travel cover for Europe for all Silver current account holders and their partners (for charges on this account, see breakdown cover on page 178) and free worldwide travel cover on its Gold, Platinum and Premier accounts. Halifax offers worldwide annual insurance with its Ultimate Rewards current account, which costs £12.50 a month. HSBC's student account comes with two years' free travel cover, while Barclaycard offers single trip travel insurance for cardholders who book a holiday through its travel service. For more details on packaged accounts and credit cards, visit www.moneyfacts.co.uk.

Beware Travel Accident Insurance

Don't be misled by the travel cover offered with some credit cards. Amex, MBNA and Co-operative are just a few of the credit cards which offer travel accident insurance – which is different from travel insurance despite sounding very similar. This type of cover only insures you against any accident that befalls you while in transit in a train, hire car or plane when you paid for the tickets or car hire using the card. It does not cover accident or illness while you are actually on your holiday and offers no cover for lost personal items or luggage.

Be Upfont

You must tell the company about any medical conditions you or your fellow travellers suffer from, regardless of who they have a travel insurance policy with. It won't necessarily increase your premiums – instead the insurer may insist that any claims arising from a pre-existing condition such as diabetes or a heart condition are excluded. But failing to mention the condition could invalidate any claim related to it. For example, if the trip has to be cancelled because a fellow traveller has a relapse of a condition from which he or she already suffers, your insurer could refuse your claim for a refund on the holiday.

Hiring a Car

Practically every airline offers car-hire deals on their websites these days, but as ever, it is worth checking out some comparison websites before you sign up for a deal. www.travelsupermarket.com is a good place to start.

Excess

 'Collision damage waiver': Buying this when hiring a car will mean you don't have to foot the bill if you have an accident or if the car is stolen. But even with this cover, if you have a collision, you may be expected to pay an excess before the policy kicks in. This excess can be as high as £1,600.

 Excess waiver: You can buy this from the car hire firm at additional cost, reducing your excess payment to near zero. But this can cost between £6 and £12 a day, adding £84 to the cost of a one-week trip and £168 for a two-week holiday. If you plan to hire a car several times in a year, or hire one for a long period of time, you may be better off by buying the excess waiver independently from a firm such as www.insurance4carhire.com, which charges £49 for an annual Europe-wide policy and £69 for a worldwide deal. These policies work by refunding any excess you are asked to pay by a car hire company.

Travel Accident Insurance

Another trick to remember when hiring a car is not to be tempted by the travel accident insurance as this type of cover is probably included in your travel insurance, or offered as a perk on your credit card (see above).

Go to the Petrol Station Before Returning the Car

Leave plenty of time when you are travelling back to the airport or car hire depot to stop off and fill the tank up with petrol. In most cases, the car hire firm will charge you more to refuel the car than you will pay on the garage forecourt.

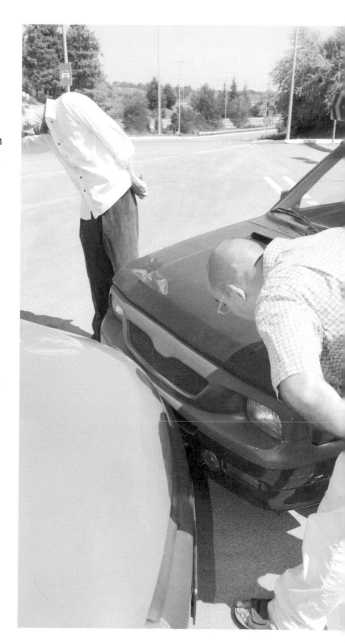

Include The Car in Your Holiday Snaps

Another good trick is to take a photo of the car when you pick it up and when you drop it off to record that you haven't done any damage to it. A couple of holiday snaps could be enough to prove that you didn't damage the car should the car hire firm later contact you to enquire about bumps or scrapes to the vehicle. Some travellers have reported that car hire firms simply debited their credit cards for damage after the event, so make sure to check your statements carefully when you return from holiday.

Train Tickets

Working out train fares in the UK is a complicated business as the array of deals on offer is sometimes mind-boggling.

Be an Early Bird

The same rule as plane tickets often applies – the earlier you book, the better deal you will get. Booking a ticket early from London to Edinburgh could cut the cost of your ticket by about £70 according to TheTrainline, a rail ticket website. Even booking a ticket on the morning of the day you travel, rather than waiting until you get to the station, can save you cash. You can search for fares on www.thetrainline.com or www.nationalrail.co.uk – but remember that TheTrainline charges a booking fee if you book your tickets online via its website. You can sidestep this fee by going direct to the train companies websites. Some train companies even offer a discount for booking online; for example, National Express offers a 10 per cent discount on rail fares booked in advance on its website.

Try Alternative Combinations to Cut the Cost

A quick way to check if you cut the cost of your ticket is to compare the cost of two single tickets rather than a return fare to your destination. As bizarre as its sounds, this can work out cheaper. If you have a bit of time on your hands, you may be able to save even more by comparing the cost of tickets if you break up your journey. For example, if you are travelling from London to Edinburgh, you could check the cost of a ticket from London to York, and then on to Edinburgh from York. Likewise, you could break up a trip from London to Penzance by checking tickets to Exeter, then on to Penzance.

Don't Pay Full Rate for Calling National Rail Enquiries

We've all been there – you can't remember what time the train leaves, so you make a quick call to National Rail Enquiries (08457 48 49 50). But this is a premium rate phone line, so will cost you more than an ordinary call. To find out alternative numbers you can call for National Rail Enquiries and other premium rate phone lines, visit www.saynoto0870.com, which lists alternative numbers beginning with local codes of 01, 02 or 03, thus cutting the cost from a premium rate call to that of a local one.

Travel Money

You can choose to take cash, traveller's cheques, prepaid cards on holiday, or you can simply use your credit card.

Taking Cash

If you want to take local currency with you, make sure you don't pay over the odds for converting your sterling. One way to ensure you get the most from your money is to order your currency in advance. Most foreign exchange outlets in airports and ferry terminals are able to offer less competitive exchange rates as they know you have little choice about where you change your money once you are en route. Both the Post Office and Marks & Spencer charge no commission on foreign currency transactions. Several organisations, such as the Post Office and Travelex allow you to order commission-free currency online. The Post Office will send the cash to you free of charge if you order more than £500. Orders for less than this will cost £5.00. If you order with Travelex, you can collect your currency at their outlets. To check out the charges levied by other currency providers, visit www.moneysupermarket.com.

Credit and Debit Cards

It may be handy to use your credit card abroad, but remember that most cards charge a foreign transaction charge each time you make a purchase. This charge is usually 2.75 per cent of the sum you spend, adding £27 to £1,000 worth of purchases.

 Credit card cash withdrawals: These can become very costly, especially if you frequently visit ATMs. Credit cards usually charge a two per cent fee starting at a minimum of £2 for cash withdrawals. To sidestep these steep withdrawal fees, you can use Nationwide Building Society's credit card or Abbey's Zero credit card as they levy no withdrawal charges. But remember, the interest charged on cash withdrawals on credit cards can be as high as 28 per cent.

Debit card cash withdrawals: Debit cards have no such interest charges, but most debit card providers also charge withdrawal fees of around £1.50 for using a foreign ATM. Again, Nationwide is the exception, offering free withdrawals on its FlexAccount debit card.

Protection: However, there is a bonus if you do use a credit card to buy goods abroad as you are automatically covered by the card provider for transactions of up to £30,000 if the goods you buy turn out to be faulty.

Prepaid Cards

These cards can be the ideal way to bring your travel money abroad. You will usually pay an initial fee when you buy the card and some cards charge an additional fee each time you top up your card with cash. The Post Office's Travel Money prepaid card charges 1.5 per cent each time you add money to the card, with a minimum fee of £3 and a maximum fee of £20. FairFX Euro Currency card does not have any loading charges.

No hassle: Unlike the hassle involved if your cash is stolen, if your prepaid card is stolen, you can simply call up the provider who will cancel the card and issue you a new one. They are safer than debit or credit cards as fraudsters can not run up huge bills on these cards.

Choose well: Be careful about which prepaid card you choose, as if you are travelling it will be easier if you can top up your card on the phone or via the internet. Not all prepaid cards have this facility. The Post Office allows you to top up your card via the telephone, while FairFX allows you to top up your card via the web. For a choice of the best cards, visit www.moneysupermarket.com.

Services & Utilities

Utilities

An easy way to save hundreds of pounds is by switching your gas and electricity supplier. You could also save money by fitting a water meter.

Gas and Electricity

Once you have found a new provider for your gas, electricity, or both, it should take up to six weeks for the switch to be made. Importantly, it's worth noting that you won't lose your supply during the switchover and contrary to popular belief moving energy supplier doesn't involve anyone coming to your home to switch you over or changing pipes or meters. Once the new supplier is set up you will need to arrange new direct debits if you pay this way.

How to Compare

Gas and electricity plans are very complicated so you should use a comparison site that is signed up to the Energywatch 'Confidence Code'. This is a voluntary code of conduct that ensures that sites are independent of suppliers and that they include details of all the available plans from all suppliers. It also ensures that sites are clear about how they make money and how savings calculations are made. For a list of sites signed up to the code see www.energywatch.org.uk. If you don't have access to the internet you can call

Energywatch on (0845 9060708) and it will send you a comparison of the prices for all the major suppliers in your area. You can also phone the comparison sites to compare plans and switch. Two of the most popular websites for energy switching are www.uSwitch.com (0800 404 7961) and www.moneysupermarket.com (0845 345 1296). Some of the sites also give information about customer service that could be a factor in which company you choose.

Online Discounts and Direct Debit

Energy suppliers reserve their cheapest prices for people who operate their account online as operating costs are cheaper. You can also save money by paying by Direct Debit. A few sites offer cashback for switches, for example, www.moneysupermarket.com, www.energyhelpline.com and www.ukpower.co.uk (all members of the Energywatch Confidence Code).

Capping

Energy costs increased dramatically in 2008 and are predicted to continue to rise in the next few years. One way of protecting yourself against future energy price rises is to choose a plan that has fixed prices. These plans guarantee that for the length of the plan the price you pay for your energy will not increase. You can normally fix prices for one or two years. Fixed price plans are more expensive in the short term, but if prices rise you will be protected against your bills increasing. During the fixed period, cancellation charges normally apply if you want to switch to a new provider. When you compare new energy suppliers compare prices for fixed prices with those of variable price plans and see how they compare. Fixed price plans are good for people who want to budget for their energy costs for a period and not be faced with higher bills if energy prices rise.

What You Will Need to Compare Energy

Which companies you can switch to will depend on who supplies your area and whether you want to include 'green' providers. When you contact your chosen supplier you will need:

 Documents: Your previous bills or details of your consumption of gas and electricity, and your address.

✅ **Current provider**: Details of your current provider and which tariff you are on to give an accurate savings calculation. This should be given on your bill.

✅ **Property details**: You may be asked questions about your property and how many people live there – this is so the site can work out how much energy you use in order to give you an accurate saving.

Water

Unlike your gas and electricity, you can't save money by switching your water supplier, but you could save money by choosing a water meter. With a water meter you pay for what you use instead of paying a flat fee. Depending on how much water your household uses you could be better off with a meter. In order to work out if you will save money you could use the calculator on www.ofwat.gov.uk – the regulator of water supplies in the UK – or uSwitch.com's calculator, which is easier to use. Once a meter is fitted, though, you only have 12 months to change your mind and switch back.

Communication

How we communicate is changing rapidly. Everyone now has a mobile and most people have access to fast broadband internet connections. You can now bundle services together and get them from the same provider. Making phone calls via the internet is now a reality. However, with this rapid change and innovation comes increasing complexity. Get it right, though, and choosing the right products from the right providers could save you money. The easiest way to compare the range of products and services on offer is to use a comparison website.

Broadband

Broadband has now pretty much replaced the slower dial-up internet, and in recent years the speed of broadband available has increased while prices have dropped. If you are still on dial-up, or haven't switched broadband provider for a few years then you could save money by switching now.

Speed of Connection

Most of the country can now get broadband, but while the speed of connections has increased overall, the speed you get will normally depend on where you live and how far you are from an exchange. A connection with a speed of 1 mb or 2 mb would be sufficient for most people, but up to 8 mb, and more, is available.

Usage Allowances

You need to take into account how much you are going to use the internet when you choose a supplier. If you use the internet a lot to download pictures and movies or online gaming, then you might need one that doesn't limit how much you can download each month or has a higher download limit. For most people 1 or 2 gb of downloads per month should be sufficient; for example, a 2 gb allowance would let you view around 50,000 web pages each month. You can pay for extra usage if you use more than this on a pay-as-you-go basis. You can also cap your usage so you don't get an unexpected bill. Broadband contracts normally tie you in for 12 or 18 months, but some let you do it monthly.

Free Routers

Some providers will give you a free or discounted wireless router when you sign up with them. This means you can access your broadband connection around your home or in the garden, on a laptop or other device with Wi-Fi.

Check the Speed of Your Connection

The speed of your broadband connection may not match the speeds quoted by broadband companies. The speed you get depends on several factors: how far you are from the exchange, how many people are using the service and so on. You can check your speed for free using one of the online speed checkers, www.speedtest.net or www.broadbandspeedchecker.co.uk.

Switching

You need to ask your existing broadband provider for a MAC code (migration authorisation code). This should mean that the switch runs smoothly – without a MAC code it could take a few weeks for your new account to be set up.

Satellite and Cable TV

There are several ways to get digital TV. Virgin Media provides cable TV along with phone and broadband. Sky Digital provides TV via a satellite dish. You can also get TV from BT with its broadband service.

What Channels Do You Need?

You need to compare the channels you want with the monthly cost. You should time the monthly cost by 12 to give you the annual cost as this can be quite high. You need to decide if you need the extra channels or you will be wasting money.

Freeview

A cheaper alternative is Freeview. You simply buy a box for as little as £15 or £20 and it gives you around 40 digital TV channels and 25 radio stations. There is no contract or monthly fee. Everyone will need to be able to receive digital TV as the old analogue service is being switched off by 2012. All new TVs now come with digital TV built in.

Comparison

The easiest way to compare digital TV is with one of the comparison sites such as, for example, www.uswitch.com, www.homephonechoices.co.uk, www.simplyswitch.com or www.simplifydigital.co.uk.

Home Phone and Mobile

Choosing who you should use for your home phone service is pretty complicated. Your options depend on who provides your landline, where you live, how many calls you make, when you make them, if you phone mobiles and landlines, and if you make international calls. Comparison sites are the best way to compare, however you will still need your wits about you and it will take a bit of time to work out which is the best option.

Calls Over the Internet

Two people can call each other for free using the internet, for example, Skype. To do this you will both need speakers and headset, or microphone, and the same software. You can also call from your computer to phones and mobiles for a charge, for example, using www.voipcheap.com or www.vonage.com.

Pay-As-You-Go v. Contract

Most people have a mobile nowadays, but are you getting the best deal? Contracts are cheaper than pay-as-you-go phones, but you are tied in for 12 or, increasingly, 18 months and often spend more than the monthly fee with extra calls and services. If you are nearing the end of your contract or it has finished already you should contact your existing phone company to see what they can offer you to keep your custom, for example, an upgraded phone or better deal. You will normally be able to choose a new phone with each contract. Or switch to get a better deal and a new phone. With pay-as-you-go you have the benefit of knowing how much you have spent each month. You aren't tied into a contract but it can be more expensive than contracts. You need to consider how long credit lasts for and what the minimum top-up is. It can be easier to get a pay-as-you-go phone if you have a poor credit rating.

How to Choose a Mobile

First you need to decide if you want a pay-as-you-go phone or a contract phone (see above).

Handset: Is there a specific handset you want? This will limit the suppliers and deals you can choose.

Minutes: How many voice minutes do you need – split between landline and mobile? How many texts do you need? And are texts rolled over from month to month? Is billing by minute or second?

Services: Do you want other services such as internet, downloads, multimedia text messages and video calling? Most people just use mobiles for phone calls and texts. If you are going to use your phone to surf the internet it will be cheaper to buy an add-on that gives you time to spend on the internet – some have unlimited plans.

Compare online: Use a comparison site to compare deals, for example, www.omio.com, www.uswitch.com, www.moneysupermarket.com, www.niftylist.co.uk.

High street: Visit high street phone stores to try phones and get information about deals.

Cashback: Watch out for companies offering cashback that you have to claim at a later date – it can be notoriously difficult to satisfy the conditions and you may not get the cashback you expect.

Get Money for Your Old Phone

If you have an old phone you no longer need you could get some cash or vouchers for it. There are several companies that will give you cash for your old phone. It needs to be in pretty good condition to get the best price, but they may consider non-working phones too. A few sites to try are www.envirofone.com, www.mazumamobile.com and www.mopay.co.uk.

Financial Services

Financial services is one area where not choosing the right product can seriously damage your financial health. For example, most people have never switched bank account and probably have the same bank account they opened when they started their first job. The banks exploit this loyalty by giving most people just 0.1 per cent interest on money in their bank accounts and charge around 15 per cent when they are overdrawn. Switching bank account is much easier than people think and although you have to have your wits about you it can be done with just a signature. You can also get a much better deal on your saving accounts, credit cards, loans, mortgages and insurance.

Bank Accounts

Switching to a new account could not only make you better off but you could get better service too.

Choosing

In order to choose a new bank you first need to work out what sort of account you need. People who normally have money in their bank account should look for an account that pays a good credit interest rate on money in their account. If you are normally overdrawn you should choose an account that has a low rate on borrowing – some accounts even offer 0 per cent overdrafts for an introductory period. Some offer an interest-free overdraft for the life of the account – however these tend to be around £100 to £250 only. To find the best bank account use a comparison site or look at newspapers. The Banking Code offers you protection if something goes wrong and sets out timescales for banks to follow. For example, all your Direct Debits and standing orders will be switched automatically to your new bank.

Avoid 'Packaged' Accounts

Check if you are paying a monthly fee for your bank account for extras like travel insurance, fraud protection, breakdown cover and access to your credit file. Unless you need and use all the benefits, and don't have them already elsewhere, you're almost certainly wasting money. When you choose a new account think very carefully before choosing one with a monthly fee.

Savings and ISAs

If you leave your money in your main bank account you could be getting as little as 0.1 per cent interest on it – this could give you just £1 on a £1,000 for a year. By opening a savings account or choosing a better bank account you should be able to earn 50 times this – giving you £50 on £1,000 for a year instead. The simplest account to open is an instant access account – this gives you access to your money whenever you want it.

If you have spare cash to save everyone should take advantage of ISAs; these are tax-free savings accounts and as a result if you are a taxpayer any interest you receive is tax-free. For 2007–08 you could invest £3,600 into a tax-free savings account.

Loans

There are two types of loan – those secured against your property (secured loans) and those without security (unsecured loans). Although loan rates have increased in the last year because of the impact of the credit crunch, you can still get a good deal and unsecured loans are much cheaper than credit card standard rates and overdrafts. It's unlikely that your bank will offer you the best deal on any of your finances, so it makes sense to shop around. Comparison websites are the best place to look, although you need to bear in mind that not all loans will be listed on all the sites. You could also check newspapers for their best-buy tables.

Unsecured Loans

Interest rates are fixed for the life of the loan – as a result your monthly repayment remains the same and at the end of the loan all of your debt is repaid. Watch out for your lender adding on expensive payment protection insurance. You can buy this much cheaper elsewhere. For example, www.paymentcare.co.uk and www.britishinsurance.com.

Secured Loans

Think very carefully before securing a debt against your property. With a secured loan your home is at risk if you can't make the repayments. Interest rates are normally variable too, which will mean your repayments can vary.

Mortgages

Your mortgage is your biggest financial commitment. However, many people have never thought about switching their mortgage and as a result could be wasting thousands of pounds. Mortgages are complicated so it's essential that you shop around carefully and get some financial advice. It's a good idea to do some research yourself by reading newspapers, looking online at sites like www.moneymadeclear.fsa.gov.uk or www.which.co.uk and get some advice from an independent financial adviser.

Fixed or Discounted Rate

If you are paying the SVR – standard variable rate – then you could save money by switching to a fixed or discounted rate mortgage. The best deals are reserved for those with larger deposits and good credit ratings but you could save money by switching. Fixed rate deals give you a fixed period for a number of years, from two to five years typically and discounted rates offer a discounted rate of say 0.5 per cent for the same sort of period. If you take out one of these deals you will normally be tied in for the length of the deal and you need to take into account fees for switching mortgage, for example, arrangement fees and legal fees. Some lenders will pay some of these fees for you when you switch to them.

Mortgage Insurance

One thing to watch out for is advisers trying to sell you insurance with your mortgage. Your mortgage is complicated enough without worrying about protecting yourself or your family. You should do this in a separate session with an adviser. One insurance you might need to think about, though, is life insurance. See life insurance, later.

Credit Cards

Choosing the right credit card can save you hundreds of pounds and even earn you money. However, you have to have your wits about you in order to choose the right card and watch out for the sneaky tricks card companies use to catch you out.

Cashback Cards

You can earn money with credit cards if you know how to play the game. With a cashback credit card you get a percentage of everything you spend on the card. However, you should only think about a cashback card if you always pay your credit card bills in full each month – so you are not using them to borrow money.

Short-Term Balance Transfers

If you have a debt outstanding on a credit card you could save hundreds of pounds transferring it to another card that offers a 0 per cent introductory rate. You could transfer the debt and not pay any interest for up to 15 months. You will have to pay a transfer fee of around 2.5 or three per cent of each transfer, but this could still save you lots of money, as credit cards charge around 17 per cent on money you've borrowed. If possible, pay off the debt in the 0 per cent period – if you still owe money at the end of the 0 per cent period switch to another credit card. It's essential that you don't use the card to make purchases – as these will be charged interest at a much higher rate.

Lifetime Balance Transfers

If you have a large debt on one or more cards you could transfer it (at a 2.5 or three per cent fee) to a credit card with a low interest rate until the debt is repaid in full. You then don't have to keep switching it from card to card and paying transfer fees. Most lifetime balance credit cards charge around five or six per cent on the debt you transfer.

Purchase Cards

Some cards give you 0 per cent introductory rates on purchases you make with the card for up to 12 months. However, you will be charged if you take cash out. Remember this isn't free cash and at the end of the introductory period if you don't repay it you will be charged the normal interest rate – average rates are around 17 per cent.

Store Cards

Store cards are best avoided as interest rates tend to be some of the highest around – up to around 30 per cent. See page 53 for more advice on store cards.

Section 75 – Useful Shopping Protection

An extremely valuable benefit of buying things on a credit card (and not debit cards) is the extra protection you get from Section 75 of the Consumer Credit Act 1974. When you buy something that costs more than £100 and less than £30,000 with a credit card and something goes wrong like the goods don't turn up or aren't as they were described you can claim your money back from the card company or the retailer.

Insurance

If you don't regularly switch insurance company you could be throwing away hundreds of pounds each year. Even when you have switched you shouldn't rest on your laurels – a good price one year doesn't guarantee a good price the next. In fact, insurers offer good deals to new customers and then put up prices once they have your custom.

Buildings Insurance

Buildings insurance covers your building against damage from fire, flood, subsidence and so on. You need to work out how much buildings insurance you need – this is the rebuilding cost and not the market value. The Association of British Insurers has a calculator to work out how much it would cost to rebuild your house (see http://abi.bcis.co.uk). If your property is at risk of flooding or subsidence, you may find it much harder to get cover and premiums will be higher. If you live in a leasehold property your managing agent will sort out the insurance and you won't be able to switch. However, you should check the policy is in place and that it is a reasonable price.

Contents Insurance

Surprisingly many people don't have insurance to cover their belongings at all or don't have enough cover. You need to make sure you have sufficient cover for all your belongings. Go round your property and make a list of all your belongings and the cost of replacing them individually. Choose a policy that offers enough cover for your belongings.

Life Insurance

Anyone who has children or people who depend upon them, for example, a husband, wife or partner, needs life insurance. If you are single and don't have any kids you don't need life insurance – no matter what an adviser may tell you. Compare premiums using a comparison site and get financial advice before you buy.

Where to Go for Insurance

The quickest and easiest way to search for cheaper insurance is to use one of the comparison websites. However, you need to be aware that they all work slightly differently, with some offering more accurate quotes based on more questions and some giving you access to more companies than others. Nevertheless, using an online site is much better than staying with your existing insurer or just buying it from your bank where you have your main bank account as it's unlikely that you will get the best deal available. Take note of the following:

☑ **What's covered?**: When comparing policies and quotes from anywhere you need to take into account what's covered by the policy and the excess with each policy. A seemingly cheap quote may be cheap because it has a higher than normal excess or doesn't have some of the cover that you really need.

☑ **Have your details**: You will need details of your no-claims discounts and details about your property, car or contents. As with all financial products it's essential that you answer all questions truthfully and tell the insurer anything you think could affect your insurance. If you don't do this and need to make a claim you could find you have less cover than you thought or not be covered at all.

Useless Insurance to Avoid

Banks also make loads of money selling expensive insurance that you don't need and probably won't ever use, such as:

☑ **Card protection**: costing £10 to £20 a year, this covers you against the loss and fraudulent use of your cards. However, you aren't liable for fraud on your cards anyway and it is a complete waste of money.

☑ **Identity theft insurance**: in the unlikely event that you are the victim of fraud, these policies, costing up to £100 year, offer you help to sort it out and cover against legal costs, as well as access to your credit file. However, it's unlikely you will ever need to use this insurance – you would be much better off buying a shredder for as little as £15, regularly checking statements and being careful how you use your card.

☑ **Credit card payment protection insurance**: this is insurance to protect the repayments on your credit card. However, it is very expensive, is of little benefit and is best avoided.

Sport & Leisure

Sport & Exercise

Using fitness facilities is usually associated with expense; the equipment can be pricey to buy and gym memberships are not any cheaper. Exercising outside is free but not always realistic when the weather is poor or if you need motivation from an instructor. For those of you needing gadgets to assist your physical workouts, you will need to be just as savvy about spending on those as if you were shopping for any other goods or services.

Best Places to Buy Sports Gear

If you are interested in setting up a home gym or even if you need golf clubs or a badminton racket check the main shops first. If the prices are too high and there is no budget option, check out the wider marketplace online.

Main Retail Shops

Retail names like JJB Sports and Sports Soccer are at the bargain end of the sports shopping spectrum and are good for purchasing brand trainers with eye-catching low price tags. Catalogue shopping companies like Argos are long-standing favourites for attractive prices and sell home fitness equipment like treadmills and fitness bikes.

Fashion

If you opt for something not out of date but out of fashion there is likely to be a sale tag on the item, meaning you have quality equipment at a bargain price – sold at a reduced cost not because they are faulty or because they aren't effective but purely because there is a newer model on the market. Choosing lesser known brands of equipment and clothes also shuts down the profit margin.

Specialist Items

Expensive items like golf clubs can be found at knock-down prices at regular chains that have a low budget appeal, especially places like Sports Soccer where you can find some equipment at half the prices you might expect. www.sportsdirect.com has a range of equipment at slashed prices and has 24-hour delivery. Similarly, www.sportsworldonline.co.uk offers some low prices on anything from darts to hockey sticks.

Gym Membership

Some of us do not want to sacrifice our gym membership so there are ways of cutting the costs. Membership does not have to equal the cost associated with an exclusive health spa, where all the pampering extras can drive up customer costs.

Negotiation

Haggling is not confined to the marketplace so don't be afraid to try it with the big chains too. Often the big health clubs offer free trials for a day or sometimes even a week, with no obligation to sign up after. If you decide to join remember they want your membership, which gives you room to negotiate a deal. Do your maths first so you can calculate how often you would need to attend the gym on a weekly basis to make it worth your while money-wise. Don't assume your local leisure centre is the cheapest option or the best value for money, although they tend to be reasonable.

Independents

If you can find an independent gym off the beaten track that isn't an exclusive club, bargaining for a better price on membership might be easier than with the market leading clubs, which could be less flexible with price structures. They will be looking to sign you up quickly so you don't choose their big name rivals instead.

Seek Out Deals

Check your local press advertisements for introductory offers and ask gym management about special off-peak prices or deals for couples. If swimming is a must, combined deals for pool and gym at local leisure centres are usually competitive. Also, check if a nearby school has a swimming pool and ask if there are public swimming times; although it is rare, it is likely to be cheap if they do.

Sports Clubs

For the more competitive sports personality sports clubs offer a team environment and often the price of using facilities is spread evenly among the team-mates. Encourage your fellow sportsmen and women to research different pitches or courts as a way of driving down overheads.

Tax Relief

If you register your club under the Community Amateur Sports Clubs (CASC) scheme you could be entitled to tax relief and gift aid options. The scheme is provided by the Government Department for Culture, Media and Sport to ensure sport and leisure is affordable around the UK.

Sports Accessories

Home video workouts, stretch mats and Pilate balls are worthwhile purchases for those wanting to exercise at home. They can be the finishing touches to your sports regime and shouldn't be avoided because you are worried about money.

Online

Before mindlessly picking them up at the first shop you go to check out the prices online, particularly for DVD home workouts, as websites like Amazon.com and Play.com might be able to offer what you need at bottom end prices. Accounts are easy to set up with a debit or credit card. Simplyswim.com sells accessories for the pool with a good range for children too and all at very reasonable to low prices.

Extreme or Specialized Sports

Some sportswear is too niche for the main locations you shop in. If you are big on skiwear, the latest in trendy skateboarding clothes or you are a major player of water sports, you do not need to sacrifice your love of sport because of cash flow problems.

Shops to Try

Some budget department stores offer brand names at discount prices, for example:

 TK Maxx: This discount store occasionally stocks specialized sportswear such as salopettes for skiing. Their range can also be up to 60 per cent less than normal retail price.

 www.outdoormegastore.co.uk: Outdoor Megastore has a massive range of clothes and equipment for outdoor pursuits with many products at affordable prices.

Sports Insurance

If you are a thrill-seeking risk taker, you will also need to purchase the right insurance at the right price to protect yourself. Similarly, sports insurance is not always automatically covered in your travel insurance so you will need to think carefully about your choices if you are combining your hobby with a holiday.

Specialized Insurance Companies

Insurance tailor-made for your sporting activities is, perhaps surprisingly, likely to be of good value compared to what some regular insurance companies offer. www.sportscoverdirect.com and X1 Sports Insurance (provided through Essential Travel Limited) both give competitive quotes.

New on the Market

Newly emerging sports insurance companies are a cost-effective option as contracts could become more sophisticated or specific and prices will be lower as the company introduces itself to potential customers.

Entertainment

At times when you have to rein in your spending and you do not have enough money to lavish on yourself, try not to think of entertainment as an obstacle in your monthly allowance. You do not have to be filthy rich to be able to enjoy a night out. If you are strict with yourself and you go to the right places at the right times, entertainment will not cost the earth. Entertainment is one of the easiest areas in which to find a bargain, especially if you live near a town or city where restaurants, bars and clubs are competing for your custom.

Nights Out

Painting the town red can cost a fortune if you let it. Drinks, snacks, club entry and a taxi dig into your disposable income. The best advice is not to give in to peer pressure and instead suggest your own ideas for an inexpensive night; chances are your friends will want to save money too.

Mid-Week Clubbing

When it comes to entertainment and clubbing nearly everything goes up in price at the weekend. If you can limit the effects of a likely hangover the next working day try enjoying a night out during the week. The entrance fee for clubs will be less painful and there are more likely to be drinks offers.

Make It Early

If going out mid-week is not an option make sure you get to your chosen venue early as the prices are often bumped up after a certain time. If you go out early you might want to go home early and be in time for the last train or bus home, which is a lot cheaper than paying for a taxi. However, if you refuse to let time be an issue on your night out, get as many friends as possible to share the same taxi. Maybe even stay at one person's house overnight to make the journey home even cheaper.

Guest List

If there is a large number of you going out it might be worth ringing the venue beforehand to see if you can get in free on a guest or VIP list. The promise of drawing in a large crowd is a good bargaining tool.

Bars with a Dance Floor

Search for a large bar that has a dance floor and a lively atmosphere and consider choosing this as your venue for the evening. Many bars will not charge an entrance fee and if they do it probably will be less than a nightclub.

Comedy

Seeing a live comedy act can be a great night out but can also be expensive. There are ways for it not to break the bank if you are willing to make certain sacrifices.

Getting Tickets Early

Big online ticket vendors like www.ticketmaster.com sometimes offer lower cost seating if you get in first when the tickets go up for sale. However, tickets for some big name comedians may only be priced at one standard rate, in which case the only way to save money is to avoid paying by credit card and having tickets delivered by special delivery, as this can add pounds to the original cost.

Comedy Membership

Signing up to comedy club membership is free at www.hahaheehee.com and ensures you receive alerts about discounted tickets and other promotions. Other venues have membership opportunities and if they charge it is still likely to be cheaper than paying for individual tickets, especially if you go to a lot of comedy nights.

Up-and-Coming Acts

Put your faith in the comedic talent of tomorrow and you could reap the rewards, in your bank account if not in your splitting sides. Although it is risky because new starters could prompt cringing rather than raucous laughter, the night will be inexpensive and some undiscovered talent could be worth more than you paid for entrance, if you were even charged a fee.

Gigs & Concerts

At some point many revellers want a night out that includes some live music but cannot always afford the ticket, let alone the extras that push our wallets to bursting point like drinks and transportation.

Keep It Local

Try going to see unsigned band nights as a cheaper alternative to paying record prices for the big bands at even bigger and more costly venues. Your local pubs or bars may charge a small entrance fee and some local gig venues will sell tickets but the amount will be inexpensive.

Combine with a Holiday

Going to see the big names in the music industry is a costly experience but you might be able to get a ticket for next to nothing if you are willing to combine the concert with a holiday. Tickets can be cheaper abroad and some online deals will practically give away the tickets if you buy a hotel and flights package deal with it. If you plan your holiday around the same time and places as your favourite acts (plus they are likely to be destinations that are pleasant to visit) the overall benefits will not break the bank. Such an offer might be found on package websites like www.lastminute.com.

Auction Websites

You might pick up an excellent deal on eBay if the seller is eager to simply get rid of the ticket and claim his or her cash back. If the timing is close and it is the day of the concert you might find money knocked off the asking price simply to make some return and ensure the ticket and money do not both go to waste.

Competitions

If you know a band you like is due to tour keep an eye out in press and magazines for competitions. As a promotional tactic many newspapers will offer free tickets for the gig or concert simply for the price of a phone call or a postage stamp.

Cinema

The cost of going to the cinema seems to increase greatly year on year, particularly as big screen entertainment has had to fend off competition from improvements in home cinema systems and the emergence of new home technology. If you can be flexible about when you attend a showing you can knock pounds off the ticket price.

Early Bird

Most cinemas have an early bird option, which might actually be more preferable. Fewer people attend the morning viewings at cinemas because it is commonly regarded as an evening activity. If you change your behavioural pattern you can see the same film as everyone else but at a portion of the normal rate and with probably with a better choice of seating.

Family Tickets and Sessions

If you are going out with your family or if you have a large party ask what the group booking rates are, as you may well get a discount per ticket for booking all together. Cinemas also tend to have family sessions on weekend mornings. The film might have been out for some time but if you haven't yet seen it the prices are very cheap so it is a shrewd purchase.

Two-for-One and Unlimited

Orange Wednesdays are an obvious choice for people with access to an Orange network mobile phone, with the weekly offer of two-for-one on tickets. However, ask your nearest cinema if they have an annual subscription fee. Cineworld sell 'Unlimited' cards for a reasonable monthly fee so if you are a frequent cinema-goer this is one of the cheapest options on tickets.

Theatre

Ticket sellers often rely on your apathy as a shopper in order to make a profit so avoid taking the easy option when you shop for a ticket. If you are willing to sacrifice an element of comfort for the love of theatre you could pick up an even greater deal.

Bargain Websites

www.lastminute.com sometimes sells tickets for half price or less and at the time of writing had a section for tickets for ten pounds. www.londontheatredirect.com also has a range of discounted tickets and for theatres at the heart of London's West End.

Standing Tickets and Restricted Viewing

Price varies with where you sit. Standing tickets are sometimes available and are given out on the day at a fraction of the price for a normal ticket. Although the view is restricted, in reality it is still good and you do not miss out on the overall performance. These are distributed for the major shows too, so you can see the big names in theatre without forking out all of your earnings.

Returned Tickets

Some theatres will sell returned tickets at a discount price if vendors have not been able to trade all of them so it is best to contact the theatre directly on the day to find out if this is likely.

Being Flexible

If you are more flexible about what show you go to see and when you see it you can shave even more off the price of going to the theatre. Matinee performances are cheaper than evening shows and a matinee is usually performed on a Saturday too if you are unable to attend a show during the week. Low budget playhouses or lesser known plays and musicals will also reduce what you pay for a ticket.

Ticket with Dinner

Look out for bargain deals on a show and dining out too. Sellers in the city where you want to see a performance may offer such packages. Online is also a good place to check for a budget bundle, with websites like www.lastminute.com and www.theatreticketsdirect.com offering

bargains on a slap-up meal with tickets. However, be aware that if you get a good price on a ticket you can drive down the cost on a meal by eating somewhere less fancy. Chain restaurants are more likely to offer deals anyway, especially if you eat off-peak. Often restaurants or cafés near theatres offer pre-theatre dinner deals so walk around the area and check for these before you order an easy option.

Dining Out

People often shun a meal out for fear of it breaking the bank. Eating in or ordering takeaway is not always the most cost-effective option. If you can be ruthless in how you research food offers and learn to recognize seasonal patterns within the food industry, eating out doesn't have to equal a hefty bill.

Elegant Dining

You can stick to a budget and still enjoy a fancy restaurant; it just means you have to be crafty in finding the offers.

Lunch Offers

Most restaurants will have a cheaper lunch deal so opt for this over dinner. It is the same food but the price is lower and will probably include two or three courses for a fixed price.

Websites with Offers

Check regional websites for reviews that come attached with offers; you might be able to get 10 per cent or more knocked off the total food bill.

New Restaurants

If you want an extra touch of class at Michelin star level research a restaurant opened by a Michelin star chef that has not yet earned its own stars, as the food is likely to be of a similar calibre.

Tourist Offers

Check tourist hot spots for information on restaurants since they are likely to have access to vouchers as a way of enticing visitors. A local tourist office or information centre might be able to offer you a leaflet that includes a discount.

Mid-Range Restaurants

Where one restaurant stands, another usually stands right next door and both want you to sit at their table. Head to a large town or city where competition among restaurant owners is great because that is where the deals are going to be.

Press Deals

Scour local, regional and national press for vouchers and check the classifieds for news of any discounts or lunchtime offers. Sugarvine.com is a great resource for finding restaurants all over the country and gives information on restaurant deals.

Happy Hour

Chain restaurants are more likely to have a two-for-one offer on meals or drinks. Happy hours are organised for otherwise quiet business hours so if you head out straight after work you are bound to find somewhere with two-for-one on cocktails or an early bird menu.

Independent Eating

Besides going out to one of the names you know try an independent restaurant. It can be hit-or-miss but a quiet little place down a side street could be a hidden gem. More than likely you will be able to find one that is affordable for you.

Seasonal Options

Consider the season when you dine out. Many towns and cities have an annual food and drink festival and the many restaurants taking part will have special festival prices. Free tasting opportunities around the city are common so find out when the next festival is nearest you and obtain a copy of the events list. Local and regional press will most likely list the events too. By joining in the festival you might be able to try out different foods and different drinks at various places for free or at a bargain price so be prepared to tour the city for your dining out experience.

Pub Food and Takeaways

Pubs are most likely to offer hearty meals at a budget rate. Look to the light lunch meals and simple foods like jacket potatoes and sandwiches to make the overall bill less worrying. Order a half pint or a small glass of wine, even better a small soft drink to share to reduce expenditure even further.

Deals of the Day

Some chains, like the successful Weatherspoon range, have deals on different days including a curry night and a steak night, often throwing in a complimentary drink with your meal.

Takeaway to Eat In

Sometimes just the experience of going out is more important than the food, in which case instead of eating at home find a takeaway where you can sit in. The food might not be the finest you have ever tried but you can sit with friends or family and enjoy your food together away from the sofa and TV.

With Friends

Arranging a dinner at a friend's house is still dining out. A group of you can dress up the occasion and make it more formal.

Tapas Theme

Agree a small fixed amount to spend, which you are not allowed to exceed and have a tapas night where each guest contributes a different dish.

Meal Deals

Big name food halls or supermarkets like Marks & Spencer, Sainsbury's and Tesco stock eating-in meal deals, which you can take to a friend's house and create a restaurant-like environment.

Party Bookings

If you decide to head out together do the research first. Ring some of the restaurants you like the look of and ask about discounts on party bookings. Some might offer a deal anyway just to secure your visit.

Leisure

Sometimes the simple pleasures in life can still cost money. From reading to trips out with visitors, everything you want to do with your day seems to cost money at some point. If you are smart but think simple, common sense will get you the prices you deserve and leisure time can be used for relaxing instead of fretting about how much you can or cannot spend.

Reading

Reading is something we should all automatically be able to access free of charge and libraries do offer us that, however in reality not everyone will find exactly what they want at their local library and will probably have to think outside the box.

Student Book Sales

You do not have to be a student to take advantage of one of the university-linked book sales but if you are a student you probably know best when and where these will be. If you are not

a student, go to the university and look for posters and noticeboards providing this kind of information. Find out when your local university is holding a freshers' week as there are likely to be sales around this time. Try a nearby university bookshop where you are not only in with a good chance of finding student prices but you could find used books at a marked down price due to general wear and tear.

Online

Play and Amazon are popular favourites for a reason. They offer an incredible range of books cheaply, some at really low prices if the book has already been used. Similarly www.thebookpeople.co.uk has some great special offers and cheap prices. If you are looking to buy in bulk you could also have the advantage of free delivery if you spend over a certain amount.

Book Clubs

Some magazines and newspapers advertise book clubs which sell books very cheaply.
The catch is you subscribe to the company and you have to buy a certain number of books
per year so it is a good option for the truly avid reader.

Charity and Thrift Shops

Charity shops up and down the country offer second-hand books for hardly any money. If you
are not searching any particular title these shops, like Oxfam, Help the Aged or PDSA, should
really be your first port of call. It is not just a matter of conscience; these really are the places
where some of the cheapest books can be found.

Tourist Attractions

Entertaining visitors or treating yourself to something beyond the norm such as visiting theme parks
or places of interest can be expensive. If you plan carefully first it could be cheaper than you think.

Visit the Website

Think of where you would like to go, for example Gulliver's Theme Parks or Alton Towers and
then look them up on the internet. Chances are they will have details about off-peak prices,
group bookings and special two-for-one deals.

Visit the Tourist Office

The tourist office is not just there to give you advice on where to go, it is also an incredible
source of offers and vouchers for the places you want to go. Visit here and stock up on all the
leaflets that have a voucher attached.

Organized Tours

Avoid turning your nose up at the idea of being just another tourist; if you join on the back of
an organized trip or a tour bus you might gain entry to a number of places for a fraction of the
price than if you went everywhere separately on your own.

Gifts

Different Ways to Gift Shop on the Cheap

Shopping for someone else can be a laborious process if it involves trawling through busy shops at peak times. If you think first about all the ways there are to shop you could save yourself time and money. We buy so many gifts each year and it takes up a lot of our financial resources but you can limit that cycle by shopping in the right places and in the right way for you.

Online

By using the internet you are reaching an incredibly wide source of gifts at unbelievably reasonable prices. Check the website you are shopping with has a secure payment method or use the PayPal system and factor the delivery charges into your budget.

Auction Websites

If you have the time to spare and you plan your gift buying in advance shopping for others on auction websites means you can bid how much you can afford. Look on eBay and others like it for a deal and remember eBay also has a 'buy it now' option on some items so if you definitely want the product and the price is cheap you will not lose out in the bidding process. Remember that looking at less popular sites than eBay could also prove fruitful if there is less competition when you bid for an item.

Websites Attached to Shops

Many big name shops will have an online service too; take a look because sometimes they offer a cheaper rate or a discount. The websites may also have a gift service, whether it is specifically designed with gifts in mind or options to dress products up as a present.

Extras to Visit

Look at www.notonthehighstreet.com as you can choose your price range and there is even a collection of items for a low budget range. www.craftmarketcorner.com has a wide range of unique gifts suitable for all sizes of bank accounts.

Home Gift Shopping

Shopping for others does not have to be a drag, especially when it can be completed without moving from the sofa. Besides shopping online you can use catalogues and even the TV to hunt a good deal on a gift.

Catalogue Shopping

Argos, Littlewoods and Empire Stores all have catalogues detailing special offers or simply low-priced items that make good gifts.

TV Shopping Channels

Quality presents at cut-price rates can often be found on TV, for example, Price Drop TV. You can pick up valuable items reduced to a low price but remember to look at the delivery price and calculate if it is still affordable or good value for money.

Supermarkets

Supermarket shopping is not just for your weekly food shop, it is also home to a number of bargain gifts waiting for you to recognize them and snap them up. Unless the supermarket is expressly for food only and has no other sections (in which case it can still be used for food gifts) supermarkets could be a one stop shop for sourcing your gifts.

Offers

Look for the treasured two-for-one or buy two and get the third free deals. It will not be long before you need to buy a gift for another friend or relative so it could be worth paying for the deal now.

Look at All Sections

You do not have to linger around the supermarkets' small gift sections; try to see all sections as an area where gifts can be found. You could find the perfect pair of novelty socks or slippers in the underwear section.

Different Kinds of Gifts

There are so many different kinds of cheap gifts on offer but sometimes it is easier to reach for the dearer options, even though you do not have to buy lavish presents to impress the person you are giving them to.

Food

Food can be a gift straight from the heart and incorporates so much variety you cannot fail to succeed with both effect and economy. Food can be one of the thriftiest kinds of present to buy and is always good for the people who already have everything and do not want clutter in the home.

Hampers

A deli would be a good initial stop on the food hamper quest as would farmers' markets. If you want to make up your own food baskets some websites offer this option, such as www.hamper.com. You can choose smaller, budget packaging and low cost snacks and drinks offering all the promise of a picnic basket at a price you choose.

Cheese Boards

Check supermarkets for pre-made cheese boards, often sold around Christmas time. Alternatively visit a local cheese deli and make up your own. Be cautious with the cheese portions so as not to overspend and be able to buy an assortment.

Electrical Goods and Gadgets

When you think of electrical goods you might think of the bulky and costly products like fridges, washing machines and wide screen TVs. Small electrical items for use around the house, or handy little gadgets can be found in all kinds of shops and online and are easy on the pocket.

Electrical Retailers

Big name electrical retailers like Comet and Dixons will no doubt have quality products on offer and look out for special sales when you can make a saving on your gift purchases. There are also small electrical items suitable as presents on offer in smaller shops you might not think of first. Pharmacy shops like Boots and Superdrug will sell more than just beauty products. Local independent electrical stores might also have a less obvious item in their stocks but which could be just what you are looking for at next to nothing in cost.

Technology Online

There are many websites dedicated to gifts and most of them will factor a love for gadgets into their business. www.findmeagift.com has a good array of office gadgets perfect for a workmate and many of them are at low prices. Be sure to factor in post and packaging when ordering from the internet. Delivery is likely to be free over a certain amount for online shopping services so bulk-buying for many people or for the next year could be a sharp move.

Entertainment

Books, CDs and DVDs are presents frequently given and with good reason. They can be cheap to buy and are usually welcomed by the person receiving them. Make sure you look for the best offers as opposed to picking them up from the obvious, easy to reach shops at a premium rate.

Internet Orders

Amazon and Play offer cheap prices for some of the big names in entertainment. Borders UK also has a special offers section.

Best Shops

WH Smith and Waterstone's are good for deals when buying more than one book and you could also pick up magazine subscriptions in gift form from shops like these. Magazine subscriptions are usually the more cost-effective option in comparison to buying one of the adventures, experience or pamper packages. The Works is generally cheap for all books.

Pre-Owned

Pick up cheaper pre-owned entertainment items from car boot sales, Blockbuster and charity shops. Just because it is second-hand does not necessarily mean it is a faulty gift.

Ethical Gifts

If you are going to give an ethical gift in the form of a donation to charity there are still presents available with a low tariff. Charity donations are designed so all people regardless of wealth can give something, so if you think this is a good gift for the right person do not be afraid of expense.

Where to Buy

Present Aid (presentaid.org) has a list of gifts categorized in different price bands so you can decide what you can afford first and then select a charitable gift. Similarly, Oxfam, Barnardo's and various other popular charities have gift options starting at low prices.

Birthdays and Anniversaries

Everyone wants their birthday to be special and you can easily make it so for your friends and family by applying some imagination. Not all birthday and anniversary gifts have to come at a great expense and there are ways to celebrate someone's day without ending up penniless.

Milestone Dates

A double figure birthday or an 18th, 21st, 30th and beyond are traditionally recognized with more notable gifts. If you can manipulate the gift so it applies meaning to the day, there is no reason for you to fork out all of your earnings on giving the most perfect and expensive gift. The most expensive item isn't always the most special or remembered.

Legal Drinking Age – Drinking Gifts

Buying two wine glasses or a pint glass and having a name engraved in the glass is an incredibly budget-wise and yet effective gift. Dress up the presentation with tissue paper and a nice box and it makes the gift more striking. Nice glasses can be bought for a small figure sum from home department stores or you can get budget glasses from a supermarket.

Jewellery

The Half Price Jewellery Store (www.halfpricejewelrystore.com) does exactly what it says on the tin. The jewellery is not cheap or fake and there are gift boxes available at cheap prices to make the presentation more effective. Alternatively you can try the mid-range chain clothes shops. Most of the shops will have an accessories section at reasonable prices. If you live near a market known for its crafts this could also be the place to find a cheap hidden bracelet or necklace.

Thoughtful Gifts

Think about conversations you have had with the birthday girl or boy and relate your gift to their aspirations. If they are looking to the future at university or in a job make the present relevant. For example, if the recipient of the gift has ambitions to be a writer, you can buy a nice-looking but inexpensive pen from any stationary shop and have their first name or nickname engraved on it.

Children's Birthday Presents

The best and worst thing about buying for children is that whatever is in fashion changes all the time. Although your presents are sometimes made redundant very quickly, children also enjoy simple and cheap presents. If you can reflect their imagination in your shopping you are safeguarded when it comes to protecting your wallet.

Small and Simple

Although a larger sized gift does not mean a larger amount to pay, often with children small and simple is likely to be cheaper. A small toy or a bag of sweets will still go down well with the child and they are cheap to buy.

Shops for Children

Buying for children can be tricky if you do not know where to shop. The best places to look include specialized children's shops like the Early Learning Centre, Woolworths and Argos cater well for children and the big supermarkets often sell a range of presents suitable for young people.

Party Food Basket

Instead of going for the biggest and best toy or the latest pricey video game, create your own children's food basket with little bags of sweets, small toys and maybe a film. This would be easy to purchase at low cost at a supermarket or large budget shop. Poundland also do good deals on sweets if you bulk buy and will have some toys. Gift wrap and party bags can also usually be found at pound stores and thrift shops, so packaging does not have to cost much extra.

Art and Stationary Shops

Places like The Works that sell budget art utensils and stationary are ideal for children. If the child is particularly creative a few paints and stencils in a party bag will go down very well. The Works sells books, many for a young audience, at a minimum cost to you.

Disney and Film Memorabilia

With every latest children's film comes a whole spectrum of memorabilia, and more than likely with hefty price tags. Looking in supermarkets for a film or online at www.play.com or www.amazon.co.uk will be cheaper than most places. Pick something small like a stationary set or a themed glass or cup instead of heading for large soft toys or a pyjama or dress up set. Look in the catalogue shops like Argos too for bedspreads and beanbags sold at a discounted rate.

Anniversaries for Others

It is important to recognize and mark dates that are important to other people such as your parents' or friends' wedding anniversary. To minimize the expense of the occasion it's possible to find the right shops on the high street and online.

Department Stores

Big department stores like Debenhams or House of Fraser are not renowned for their budget appeal but they should not be written off as too dear either. Depending on what you are looking for they sometimes offer a bargain. Photo frames, glasses and gadgets can all be found at budget-wise prices. If you aim to go and buy these sorts of gifts in advance when there is a sale on you will have change enough for the card too.

Personal Anniversaries

Sharing an anniversary with a loved one can be really romantic. There is no need to make it a commercially overstated event, instead it can be a meal between two with small or practical gifts. If you do want to go all out for once, you can be smart about getting more for your money with what you choose to do.

Joint Present

If you cannot really afford to give each other luxurious gifts and money is tight, buy something together that you both need. Shop in budget home stores like Quality Save and Instore for a household item that needs replacing or for a new set of towels and sheets to replace some old ones. Look for something in the home that needs replacing and buy something new as a joint gift to both of you.

Combination Present

Double up your anniversary with your annual holiday. It is a great gift to enjoy together instead of buying a token, but ultimately wasteful, present. Look on www.teletext.co.uk, lastminute.com or budget airline websites like www.ryanair.com and www.easyjet.com for a last minute get away deal.

Christmas

This is the time of year when people usually write a blank cheque for the month of December and consider the whole celebration as a reason to excuse themselves when it comes to debt. However, think outside the box and be inventive with your purchases and you will be rewarded with bright smiles, grateful reactions and a bank balance that is intact. If you find the right places to buy quality but simply priced offerings you will no longer dread Christmas as the money draining season it can be for so many people.

Family Presents

Usually the biggest and best Christmas presents go to family members. Thinking small is probably appropriate if you have a particularly large family but for a reasonable number of relatives the job does not have to be as hard as you might think it is.

Practical Gifts

Supermarkets such as ASDA, Tesco and Sainsbury's all have practical gift options at prices barely noticeable hidden in your weekly food shop. Budget European supermarkets like Lidl and Aldi are also excellent for the occasionally useful household item like smoothie machines or small meat grills. Instead of buying a showy present that could see you bankrupt choose a practical and economical purchase from a supermarket or cheap home store.

Vouchers

Tokens and vouchers can appear more thoughtful than an envelope of money. Dedicating those gift vouchers for a night out on the town could be even more exciting for the person receiving your present. Lastminute.com sells theatre tokens and restaurant vouchers from a low starting price. There are also two-for-one deals and many adventure and experience gift options for those with a spending limit. Many other such websites exist where you can pick up gift experience vouchers.

Presents for Friends

It is only right that close friends want to be generous to each other at such a festive time of the year but make sure you are not buying for the sake of it and instead buy for those friends truly close to you. Cards and sweets will more than suffice for a wider circle.

Bulk Buying

This method of shopping always tightens spending output and is a good idea for large groups of friends, work colleagues and extended family members. Supermarkets and pound stores are good for this, especially for food items like sweets and chocolates. Consider buying a large case of wine, either from food halls like Marks & Spencer or from online merchants. www.laithwaites.co.uk has a 'Bin Ends' section where they drop the price on cases of wine once stocks run low. Vouchers and gift options are also available.

Small Gifts and Secret Santa

It can be hard to buy small but there are tiny gifts with tiny prices to be found in the largest of shops and department stores. Look for a 'gifts' or 'home' section within a shop but do not forget simple ideas like socks, ties and accessories which can be bought as gifts at low prices. Nearly anything can be a gift if you bestow it right. Depending on the situation, organize a secret Santa scheme at Christmas so everyone can buy one small gift as opposed to everyone buying many at great cost.

Alternative Shops

Chances are everyone will look for the special deals in the main shops and even if they haven't bought the gifts they may well have spotted them. Imagination can be vital in giving the best received presents, so look for even smaller prices at some of the more original alternative shops.

Market Shopping

If you know a good market for crafts, jewellery or food it could be a really good source of unique but well-priced gifts. Often people will assume markets are dirty or cheap in quality but this is not the case and often have some great gift ideas on sale.

Weddings and House-Warmings

It is no secret weddings can cost a fortune not just if you are the one getting married but simply if you are a guest. Similarly, helping your friends and family find their feet in a new home can be expensive depending on what you buy them. However, if you can try to be crafty in your approach you could reduce the effect of the event on your purse strings.

Wedding Lists

If you are restricted in what you buy and where you shop because of a wedding list it can be tough for people trying to control their expenditure but there are a couple of ways to avoid paying over the odds.

Get in Early

Find out when guests can start making purchases from the list and be first in line to choose your gift – that way you can select one of the lower cost items.

Join with Others

If you simply cannot afford a gift from the list check if there are other guests in your situation who might like to join forces and buy a gift together.

Money Contributions

Money contributions instead of gifts are increasingly popular for couples looking to enjoy a special honeymoon or to give to charity. Giving money gifts can be awkward if you have only a little to spend but do not want to appear ungenerous. However, a few tricks could help you out of a sticky situation.

Money with Meaning

If you can only offer quite a small amount add meaning to the numbers, for example, a pound for every day/month/year the couple have known each other. Maybe you could make it a certain amount for how long you have known the couple; at least it shows some thought and sentiment on your part.

Contributions Over Time

Be the first to buy your friend a drink at their stag or hen do and send flowers or a bottle of wine between the night out and the wedding. Consistency is also generosity, as opposed to a small one-off contribution to the wedding fund. Couples will remember this despite your small initial donation.

House-Warming

Kitchen tools and electrical equipment can come at some expense to you. It is important not to overlap with other givers or end up buying something the couple or housemates will not use. There are ways to make a fuss of your relative's or friend's new nest without paying too much.

Perishable Presents

One way to make sure you do not buy something that will be made redundant or something that clutters the place is to give a present with a short shelf life. Small scale food baskets, cheese boards and cakes or pastries are not pricey and make a nice gift, especially if the recipients are too busy unpacking to cook.

Bottle of Wine

A simple bottle of wine is a popular celebratory gift and it does not have to come from the top shelf to taste good. Oddbins and Threshers might have special deals on selected brands but also check the discount alcohol retailers like Bargain Booze for a nice wine at a markdown charge.

Thank-You, Gesture and Celebratory

It is possible to find the right gift that says 'thank you' or 'sorry' without making money the main expression of your gesture. There are many reasons why a gift is necessary, such as peace offerings, end of year presents for teachers and offerings for a host who had you to stay. Some people could be tempted to go all out and spare no expense. Sometimes it is also easier to find something that costs a lot but takes no time to find. There is no need to make the search complicated and you can save the extra cash for the next gift you have to finance.

Thank-You Gifts

The amount of cash you spend does not have to be proportional to your gratitude to someone. Most likely they will be happy you thought of them, so it is more important to make the present thoughtful.

Small Gift Shops

Something small and unusual from a small gift shop is a simple enough way to get your sentiment across and is unlikely to break the bank. There are likely to be smaller scale shops in small towns or in quieter areas of a larger town or city so try to move away from the crowds.

Charity and Thrift Shops

Not everything from charity shops is worn or second-hand. Big name charity shops like Oxfam

have some great gift ideas from fair trade chocolate and accessories to charity gifts like buying school equipment for children in developing countries.

Baby Shower, Christening and Naming Ceremonies

A new baby causes a lot of fuss and requires a lot of funding. Everybody needs to chip in but your limited wealth does not have to crash because of the event.

Gifts for the Future

The fact children grow very fast can work in your favour. When shopping for a present, if there is something that suits your budget but which is too old for the child it can be bought and offered with the child's future in mind. There will be a lot of gifts for the child in the present but less for when the baby gets bigger. Check Mothercare and the Early Learning Centre for sale items or discount offers regardless of age.

Simple Ideas

Soft toys, baby food and nappies are all items a parent will need and are less costly to buy. Often these will be the most practical of gifts; you do not need to be extravagant to give a good gift.

Further Reading

Aziz, A. and Khanzada, M., *How To Save Money on Car Insurance*, AuthorHouse, 2007

Clark, D. and Unterberger, R., *The Rough Guide to Shopping with a Conscience*, Rough Guides Ltd, 2007

Coleman, A., *Car Boot Sales: A Sellers' and Buyers' Guide*, Hallamshire Publications Ltd, 1998

Collier, M., *eBay Bargain Shopping for Dummies*, John Wiley & Sons, 2003

Davidson, P., *The Shopaholic's Top 1000 Websites: Your Guide to the Very Best Online Shopping*, Capstone, 2008

Davidson, P., *The Shopaholic's Guide to Buying Gorgeous Gifts Online*, Capstone, 2007

Fields, D. and Fields A., *Baby Bargains*, Windsor Peak Press, 2007

Finney, K., *How to Be a Budget Fashionista*, Ballantine Books, 2006

Furnival, J., *Smart Saving*, Hay House Inc, 2007

Hopkinson, N., *The Online Connoisseur*, Marlowe & Co., 2007

Kershman, A.R., *Bargain Hunters' London: All the Best Places in London to Find Great Deals*, Metro Publications, 2007

Levene, T., *The Money-saving Handbook*, Which? Books, 2008

Lewis, M. (ed.), *Thrifty Ways For Modern Days*, Vermilion, 2006

Lewis, M., *The Money Diet: The Ultimate Guide to Shedding Pounds Off Your Bills and Saving Money on Everything!*, Vermilion, 2005

Lipper A. and Lipper J., *Baby Stuff*, Marlowe & Co., 2002

Meurs, T. van, *Designer Bargains in Italy*, Editoriale Shopping Italia, 2007

Miller, M., *Bargain Hunter's Secrets to Online Shopping*, QUE, 2004

Mulvey, C., *The Good Shopping Guide: Certifying the UK's Most Ethical Companies and Brands*, Ethical Marketing Group, 2008

Mulvey, C., *The Good Shopping Guide to Renewable Energy: Your Guide to Renewable Energy, Your Guide to Saving Energy*, Ethical Marketing Group, 2004

Odulate, F., *Shopping for Vintage*, Quadrille Publishing, 2008

Phillips, B., *Teach Yourself Thrifty Living*, McGraw-Hill, 2007

Self, J., *The Teenager's Guide to Money*, Quercus, 2007

Shoop, F., *How to Profit from Car Boot Sales*, Remember When, 2009

Spencer's Labels for Less, West One Publishing, 1999

Stouffer, T., *The 'Everything' Budgeting Book*, Adams Media Corporation , 2008

Webb, B. and Heck, M., *The Mom's Guide to Earning and Saving Thousands on the Internet*, McGraw-Hill Companies, 2006

Williams, A.M., Jeppson, P.R. and Botkin, S.C., *Money Mastery: How to Control Spending, Eliminate Debt and Maximise Your Savings*, Career Press, 2002

Wilson, A., *The Consumer Guide to Home Energy Savings: Save Money, Save the Earth*, New Society Publishers, 2007

Zalewski, A. and Ricks, D., *Cheap Talk with the Frugal Friends*, Starburst Publishers, 2001

Websites

This is just a selection of some of the many useful websites discussed in the book.

Appliances and Electricals

www.appliancesonline.co.uk
www.buyersandsellersonline.co.uk
www.comet-clearance.co.uk
www.computerbargains.co.uk
www.digitaldirect.co.uk
www.discount-appliances.co.uk
www.empiredirect.co.uk
www.hugesdirect.co.uk
www.maplins.com
www.pcworld.co.uk
www.teleland.co.uk

Cashback

www.cashbackkings.com
www.greasypalm.co.uk
www.pigsback.com
www.quidco.com
www.rpoints.com
www.topcashback.co.uk
www.wepromiseto.co.uk

Clothes and Accessories

www.asos.com
www.boohoo.com
www.catwalktocloset.com
www.dailycandy.com
www.koodos.com
www.secretsales.com
www.styleshake.com
www.latestinbeauty.com

Household

www.exshowhousefurniture.com
www.Furniture123.co.uk
www.gooddealdirectory.co.uk
www.homesandbargains.co.uk
www.national-brands.co.uk
www.tradeleftovers.com
www.trade-secret.co.uk
www.showhomewarehouse.co.uk
www.whatdoidowiththis.com

Leisure

www.hahaheehee.com
www.lastminute.com
www.ticketmaster.com

Money General

www.moneyfacts.co.uk
www.moneymadeclear.fsa.gov.uk
www.moneysavingexpert.com
www.saynoto0870.com
www.which.co.uk

Price Comparison

www.confused.com
www.kelkoo.co.uk
www.mysupermarket.co.uk
www.pricerunner.co.uk
www.uk.shopping.com
www.uSwitch.com

Shopping General

www.amazon.co.uk
www.carbootjunction.com
www.craigslist.org
www.eBay.co.uk
www.gumtree.com
www.uk.freecycle.org

Travel

www.Airmiles.co.uk
www.nationalrail.co.uk
www.petrolprices.com
www.teletext.com
www.thetrainline.com

Utilities

www.energyhelpline.com
www.energywatch.org.uk
www.ofwat.gov.uk
www.ukpower.co.uk

Vouchers

www.couponsurfers.co.uk
www.myukdiscountcodes.com
www.myvouchercodes.co.uk
www.sendmediscounts.co.uk
www.totallyfrugal.com
www.ukfrenzy.co.uk
www.vouchercodes.com

Index